HOW TO GET YOUR TEACHING IDEAS PUBLISHED

A
WRITER'S GUIDE
TO EDUCATIONAL PUBLISHING

JEAN STANGL

WALKER AND COMPANY
New York

First published in the United States of America in 1994 by Walker
Publishing Company, Inc.

Published simultaneously in Canada by Thomas Allen & Son Canada,
Limited, Markham, Ontario

Library of Congress Cataloging-in-Publication Data
Stangl, Jean.
How to get your teaching ideas published : a writer's guide to
educational publishing / Jean Stangl.
p.   cm.
Includes bibliographical references and index.
ISBN 0-8027-1284-3. —ISBN 0-8027-7412-1 (pbk.)
1. Educational publishing—United States.   2. Education—United
States—Authorship—Marketing.   I. Title.
Z479.S76   1994
070.5—dc20   93-31579
CIP

The form on page 18 is reprinted with permission from *Learning93* magazine
copyright © 1993, Springhouse Corporation, 1111 Bethlehem Pike,
Springhouse, PA 19477. All rights reserved.

The material on page 144 is from *Instructor*, May 1991. Copyright © 1991
by Scholastic Inc. Reprinted by permission.

Printed in the United States of America

2   4   6   8   10   9   7   5   3

For Steve, Ken, and Bruce—
my best teachers

CONTENTS

Appendix

FOREWORD

AT LAST! HERE IS A BOOK I WISH HAD BEEN AVAILABLE
fifteen years ago when I was writing for the educational market.
In those days most educational projects were developed in-house
and were often written by in-house or long-term contracted writers. It was a hard market to break into, made even more difficult
by the paucity of information on names, addresses, and needs of
companies publishing educational materials.

At last! Here is a guide to writing and illustrating educational
material by someone seasoned and scarred by the writing and marketing wars, someone with the firsthand experience one can
achieve only after years of researching, writing, and selling. Jean
Stangl's education will serve us well as we strive to educate others.

Children deserve the very best. Parents will demand it, publishers will seek it, and authors and illustrators must deliver it. If you
can meet the challenge, then publishers will purchase your writing. Above all, you must approach whatever you do in a professional manner. Your education in the field begins with this book.
Let it be your guide throughout your career.

At last! Here is a book that doesn't try to tell you that writing for children is easy, for it isn't. Yet for those who use this book as if it were a course in developing and marketing educational materials, things will go easier, pitfalls will be avoided, and time-consuming mistakes will be minimized.

In the end, of course, it's the children using your learning aids who will benefit most.

For those of us who write for children, there can be no greater reward than knowing that something we wrote made a difference in a child's life. The more knowledge we can gather, the better our own work will be. Here then is a new book that will make a difference not only in the way we write and illustrate but also in the lives of our readers. At last!

—*Stephen Mooser, children's book author, educational materials writer, president of the Society of Children's Book Writers and Illustrators*

PREFACE

FINALLY, HERE IS A BOOK TO HELP TEACHERS FIND out how to sell their innovative teaching ideas and materials to a publisher.

As a teacher your ideas are fantastic! You have developed and tested materials that are not yet on the market. This book will help you turn those ideas into published books, teacher resource guides, and classroom learning aids.

Don't keep your ideas to yourself; share them with your colleagues, see them in print, and get paid. Writing for the educational market is a lucrative field and more open to you today than ever before.

Discover the areas in the educational market that are open to free-lance writers, who the publishers are, and now you can write and sell to them.

If you have teaching materials and/or ideas you want to see published, *How to Get Your Teaching Ideas Published: A Writer's Guide to Educational Publishing* is a book you can't do without.

- What can I sell?
- Where can I find a guide on writing for this market?
- How do I develop my ideas so they are publishable?
- Where can I find the names and addresses of publishers?
- How do I contact a publisher?
- How do I submit material in a professional manner?
- How do I write a proposal?
- How do I get paid?

The answers are in this book—the only book of its kind to thoroughly cover this genre.

Although written for the novice writer in simple step-by-step progression, the established writer who may wish to write for this genre will also find it to be a helpful, informative guide.

The main focus of the book is on infant/preschool through the sixth grade; however, the major topics are also relevant to those writing at the junior high and high school level.

When I speak at schools, the students usually ask two questions: "How old are you?" and "How much money do you make?" When I speak to students in my classes or other adult groups, they have two entirely different questions. Their main concerns seem to be, "How do I know someone won't steal my idea?" and "Do I have to provide illustrations?"

This unique guide to educational writing and publishing will tell you the approximate payment you can expect from selling magazine items, teacher resource books and aids, audiovisuals, and other supplemental materials for students and teachers. An overview is given on the copyright law, and you will discover why you do not need to copyright your ideas or materials. No, you do not need to provide illustrations—unless you are an illustrator and wish to provide them. This book does *not* tell you how old I am!

Anyone can write a book—I know this is true, as I (and thousands of others) have done so. *How to Get Your Teaching Ideas Published* tells you how to go about the process of developing your ideas into books, products, or magazine articles and starts you on your way to becoming a professional, published educational author!

ACKNOWLEDGMENTS

WHEN I FIRST STARTED WRITING FOR THE EDUCA-tional market, I discovered there was very little available in print to guide a writer in this field. This book is the result of my attempt to answer the questions asked over the past few years by students in my writing classes.

One cannot bring a book of this kind to its completion without the help of others. I wish to thank all of the following who were willing to answer questions and provide information in their area of expertise: Sandra Arnold, Susan Campbell Bartoletti, Vivian Dubrovin, Penny Holland, Rita Milios, Ginger Murphy, Walt Shelly, Carolyn Trotter, and Ernie Valdez.

And it is with deep gratitude that I acknowledge Mary Kennan Herbert, my editor—editors are very special people, but she is that *one* in a million. Thank you, Mary!

HOW TO GET YOUR
TEACHING IDEAS
PUBLISHED

1

An Introduction to the Educational Market

No DOUBT YOU ARE A CREATIVE AND INNOVATIVE person—teachers usually are. Perhaps you are a teacher or former teacher who loves to write and has the urge to put some teaching ideas into written form. Maybe you are a writer with a special interest in education, or maybe you are a school volunteer with some ideas to share—ideally in classrooms everywhere! For any of you who would like to profit from one or more of your successful teaching ideas, this is the book to help you get going. Your materials, developed and improved by you, have been classroom tested. Through your observation of students you have discovered new ways to introduce, reinforce, review, and individualize areas of the curriculum.

After revising and testing, you now feel you have something special that would be of interest to other teachers and would make learning more interesting for students. But you wonder how you should go about trying to persuade a publisher to invest time and money in your product. *How to Get Your Teaching Ideas Published: A Writer's Guide to Educational Publishing* will show you how. In the appendix, you will find a more comprehensive market list of educational publishers than you will find in any other book on the market.

There are many how-to books available on writing both for the adult and the juvenile market, but few of these mention the educational market. Lists of publishers, editors, and brief guidelines are readily available from several sources. There are many educational-writing opportunities for authors. Although I have been published in several other genres, for me, the educational market has been one of the most exciting and rewarding experiences of all.

The educational category provides an opportunity to work in many different media, to recycle your research material, and to work on several projects at the same time.

Who Can Write for This Market?

Age is no barrier, and it is never too early or too late to start. An eighty-year-old retired teacher probably has many ideas to share and would find this to be a way to continue contributing to the education of our children. A new teacher who is filled with excitement and enthusiasm may be overflowing with innovative ideas that would make teaching and learning easier for today's special instructional needs. In the course of my writing, no editor has ever asked my age. It is the uniqueness of what you have to offer, how determined you are to sell it, how well informed you are about the current market, and your ability to convince the editor, through a well written proposal, that this is a book that needs to be published. Then you must meet your deadline as you strive to write in a manner that will require as little editing and rewriting as possible.

It is not always necessary to be or to have been a teacher, although a few publishers do require it. Actual experience in the classroom is obviously very helpful. You need to have an understanding of child development, age level abilities, and what is being taught at different grade levels. Many publishers will accept free-lance work from authors who have expertise in a particular field.

If you have no teaching experience, I recommend that you volunteer on a regular basis at a local school, and work in a classroom for the age level for which you wish to write. As a teacher's aide, tutor, or volunteer, you will not only gain helpful information from both the teacher and the students but also will be given an opportunity to try out some of your ideas.

What Can I Sell?

The educational market is a rapidly expanding and profitable one for today's writers. Possibilities are almost unlimited. The educational market includes, but is not limited to, textbooks, teacher manuals, resource books, workbooks, student materials, audiovisuals, computer programs, and manipulatives for classroom students (see the options listed in the appendix on pages 181–211).

Some areas are highly specialized such as textbooks, which may take three years or more to research and write, especially high school and college textbooks. Writing elementary educational materials usually takes less time and is a field that is wide open for the solo free-lance writer. This market is also very receptive to illustrators, artists, and photographers.

Publishers pay either on a royalty basis or as a "work for hire" assignment. Some educational publishers accept proposals from free-lance writers, others give only assignments for projects created in-house.

There are over 75,000 public and private elementary schools in the United States, and they all use supplementary educational materials. Someone has to come up with new ideas, and then someone has to write these classrooms materials for the educational publishers—it could be you!

D's and P's for Authors

Writing cannot be taught, but it can be learned. If you want to learn how to write, you must have (or develop) what I call the three "D's"—desire, determination, and dedication.

1. *Desire*—You have to seriously want to write, and the desire

has to be strong enough to motivate you to write. Writing is like an addiction; it is something you have to do.

2. *Determination*—You need to be determined that you are going to write and rewrite and rewrite until your manuscript is the best you can make it.

3. *Dedication*—You must be dedicated to the craft of writing, for writing is a craft as well as an art. If you are truly devoted to writing, it will be one of your top priorities.

Likewise, if you want to get your work published, you must incorporate into your writing life the four "P's"—passion, professionalism, patience, and persistence.

1. *Passion*—You must have or develop a strong desire to get your material published. That is your main goal—to see your material in print. For you, writing is not just a hobby or something you will work on when you have nothing else to do, it is a part of your everyday life. Getting published is the purpose for your writing. You tell yourself "I am going to get published," and then work until you do.

2. *Professionalism*—Be professional.

1. Study the publisher's catalog and guidelines.
2. Follow the guidelines for submissions.
3. Use an acceptable manuscript format.
4. Spell the name of the editor and the company correctly.
5. Self-edit before mailing all correspondence.
6. Send a clear, clean copy.
7. Send your manuscript or proposal to a company that accepts your type of material.

Your chances are far better if you write a well-crafted manuscript and submit it in a professional manner. Show professionalism in your query and cover letter as well: There are certain acceptable standards and formats one needs to become familiar with and then follow. A professional manuscript is more than just a good idea.

Passion may be inborn, but professionalism can be learned.

3. *Patience*—You need to have patience not only with yourself but also with editors and even your mail carrier. You may have to wait up to three months for a response to a query. It will probably

take six months to a year to complete your manuscript, then it will be another eight to twelve months before your book is published. And another six to twelve months before your first royalty check arrives. The business of writing is a waiting game, but don't sit idly by becoming more and more impatient—start your next book or magazine article!

4. *Persistence*—No one succeeds without it. An editor is not going to come knocking on your door asking you to write an article or a book. Seldom will you get a contract from the first publishing house you query. Don't give up; keep trying—rewriting and revising if necessary and studying the markets until you find the right publisher for what you have to offer.

If you have the passion, exercise professionalism, cultivate patience, and develop a persistent attitude, you can write, you can get published, and you can make money!

Don't be a procrastinator! There is no better time than right now if you are serious about writing and selling what you write. Don't wait until the children grow up, you quit work, or your husband retires, for you won't have any more time then than you do right now.

If one waits for the right time to write, the "write" time never comes. You have already taken the first step. You bought or borrowed this book and you are reading it.

Questions Kids Ask

When I speak to schoolchildren, their two favorite questions seem to be, "How old are you?" and "How much money do you make?"

I answer the first question with, "I was over fifty when I started writing, and I was a grandmother." Somehow this seems to satisfy them.

It is probably not too realistic to think that the majority of us can make an adequate living writing full time for the children's market, except perhaps in the educational field. However, there are those prolific writers, award winners, and highly acclaimed authors and/or illustrators who write children's picture books, novels, and nonfiction who do support themselves and their families *very* well.

I truly believe the educational market is where the money is. In some cases, royalties may not be as high as in commercial publishing, but there is a greater volume of sales over a longer period of time. A book of activities to help kids learn math may ultimately sell far more copies than a novel.

I heard an editor from a well-known publishing house say that the average life of most picture books for children is five to ten years; fiction novels for the middle grades is three to five years; and young adult novels (often called "YA") is from two to three years. Nonfiction usually stays in print longer than any of these categories. Some educational materials have indefinite shelf life. I have a copy of a teacher-aid book that has been in print over thirty years, and the author still receives royalties.

After six months on the market, most juvenile books go on the publisher's "back list." Educational publishers don't have rigid back list categories. As long as the book is selling it is listed in the current catalog. The thirty-year-old book I mentioned is still in the publisher's catalog.

The average first printing for picture books is 7,000 to 10,000 copies; however, a teacher resource book may sell as many as 25,000 copies the first year. There will always be new teachers and new students and a need for new materials.

Questions from Adults

When I speak to adult groups, they have two entirely different questions than young students do. Their concerns often are, will they have to provide illustrations, and how can they be sure someone won't steal their ideas?

Most of the time, you do not need to be concerned about artwork. Editors take care of providing an artist or illustrator. You, as the author, need only to write the book. If, however, you are an illustrator or can do line drawings and wish to provide the artwork, this can usually be worked out with your editor.

No legitimate publisher is going to steal your ideas. They are always looking for new and fresh ideas as well as new authors. Publishers are in the business of making money. They make money by publishing and selling books and are not going to risk the threat of a lawsuit over a manuscript. However, since ideas cannot be copyrighted, others may have the same or similar ideas as you. Don't let fear prevent you from seeking a publisher; if your ideas are good, they will be bought not stolen.

I have divided the educational market into five major categories—books, nonbook materials, curriculum-related books, educational magazines, and the religious educational market. At first you will be more comfortable concentrating in your special area of interest, then you may want to "spread your wings" and try other options.

No one has more great ideas than a teacher. It has been said that we all have at least one book within us, and after you write one, you will discover that there are other brilliant ideas inside your head just waiting to pop out and be put on paper.

Writing and then selling your ideas for educational materials to a publisher is another avenue for teachers and others to share ideas, experience, and expertise with both adults and children and to get paid for doing it. Schools need your ideas. So, go ahead, try it!

2

Analyzing the Market

ANYONE CAN WRITE A BOOK; SELLING IT IS THE hard part. Yes, it is true that writing a magazine article or even an entire book is not unduly difficult if you are determined to do it; however, in order to interest a publisher, your manuscript must be written in a professional manner. It is also equally if not more important to study the educational market to determine publishers' interests. Each publishing house has its own special market needs. You need to find out what is already available, decide how your idea differs, and discover what might be missing in the area in which you desire to write. You do this by studying the market and scouting out potential competition.

Where Educational Materials Are Sold

Here are five major ways in which educational publishers are likely to market their educational materials.

1. *Direct Mail*—Some publishers and manufacturers print catalogs or brochures and distribute these directly to school systems

and libraries throughout the nation and in some cases in Canada and Great Britain. The school then orders directly from the publisher.

2. *Distributors*—They act as the middleman and buy large quantities of educational products directly from the publisher or manufacturer. They in turn print catalogs and sell to the schools. Distributors play an important role in sales, for if they do not buy your product it may never be seen in schools.

I was told by the editor of one company I work with that 80 percent of their books are sold to a distributor.

3. *Direct Sales*—Manufacturers, distributors, and large companies may have salespeople or sales representatives who make presentations at schools and educational conferences and conventions. Some also have experts who do workshops on perhaps science, reading, or motor development. These presentations are free, as they provide opportunities for the company to present related materials or to introduce new products.

4. *Educational Supply Stores*—Teacher supply stores, children's bookstores (these usually have a special section for teacher materials), and toy stores sell to schools as well as individual teachers. Other retail stores also stock selected materials, especially activity and learning readiness books and educational toys.

5. *Educational Conferences*—Conference and convention centers have large open rooms where they rent out booth space to publishers, manufacturers, and retailers who set up displays of books, learning materials, games, toys, and other products. They may give away free catalogs, tote bags, calendars, and other items. Educational conferences are important to a publisher or manufacturer, for this is one of the best ways to find out the reaction and interest of educators. When you attend a professional conference, be sure to pick up those free tote bags and then start filling them with publishers' catalogs. Some of the major educational organizations that hold annual or semiannual conferences are: ACEI (Association for Childhood Education International), ACSI (Association of Christian Schools International), NAEA (National Art Education Association), NSTA (National Science Teachers Association). See the appendix for a more complete list.

Where to Start

If you are teaching, start by looking through your school's educational supply catalogs. Companies, too, often advertise in teacher magazines and offer free catalogs. Go through these magazines and send for as many publishers' catalogs as possible.

Learning about various kinds of products being developed in the educational field will make you better informed about what is on the market, who some of the publishers are, and what you can sell. Studying publishers' catalogs can give you new ideas as well as ways to improve your working idea or perhaps a new way to slant your material in order to make it more appealing than what is already on the market. What you offer a publisher must be unique in some way—easier to use, more exciting for students, slanted in a new way, or simplified for younger children.

Visit local school resource libraries and school textbook libraries. Browse through the teacher supply stores in your area. Check for names of publishers, which publishers' materials the store carries, and the greatest number of titles, and make an effort to get to know the store managers. They can provide you with valuable information about the market and different products and publishing houses.

When you take a vacation or a trip to another area, set aside time to visit children's bookstores and educational supply and teacher materials stores. Check the Yellow Pages for names and addresses and make a list of the ones you want to visit. When I visit a new city, I set aside plenty of time for exploring these places.

Keep a list of the libraries, bookstores, and teacher supply stores you visit. They will be good prospects for handling your product when it is ready to market.

If you are not familiar with your state curriculum, you can write your state's Department of Education and ask for any information available on the curriculum category or grade level of your interest. If you can, find out which curriculum areas are being funded by the federal government. Although the areas and amounts change yearly, special, bilingual, and vocational education, reading, literature, and gifted programs may be possibilities. Publishers watch federal spending closely, realizing that usually money is made available where there are special needs.

Resource People

Become a frequent visitor at your public library and, if feasible, your local college library. Get to know the children's and the reference librarians, and tell them about your project. The reference librarian can help you find sources of information you never knew existed. Since most librarians are extremely busy, you might consider taking the children's librarian to lunch to talk about possible gaps in curriculum-related books. Librarians also know what students ask for in doing research projects, what is and what is not available, which subject titles are limited, and if there are any titles on the subject for a particular age group.

You will also want to develop a good relationship with school librarians and reading and media specialists at local schools, who can often offer suggestions. Later they may be willing to read, or even edit, your finished manuscript.

If you are not teaching, you will need to stay in touch with what is happening with the school curriculum. If you have time, volunteer on a regular basis to work in the classroom at the grade level in which you wish to write. You can learn a great deal by working in the classroom for two or three hours at a time. Talk to the teacher about your idea and ask if you can test it with the class. Actual classroom testing is essential to support your credibility and the validity of activities. You need to prove that your ideas will work!

Since my teaching experience included only preschool through first grade, while doing graduate work and not teaching I substituted in three different districts and volunteered on days I wasn't called to work in other grade levels. Then I proposed and taught a summer, hands-on science class for fourth through sixth grade. This class later became the basis for two science books I wrote for this age level.

Read Educational Journals and Periodicals

It is important to become well acquainted with the educational media. If you are a writer who is not a teacher, I recommend that you read *Instructor, Creative Classroom, Learning,* and as many educational journals as possible to find out what is popular or important in teaching and classroom methods. The key journals in the field will be available in the education library or collection at colleges and in many public libraries. See the appendix for a list of educational magazines.

Write It Down

Don't rely on your memory no matter how good it is. Get in the habit of keeping a journal or notebook, because if you want to be a writer you must train yourself to write things down. Write down the names of librarians and information they provide, editors or salespeople you meet at conferences, a new magazine, dates for forthcoming educational events, and contact people you meet at teachers' workshops.

Clip and file items from newspapers, magazines, and professional journals and catalogs that relate to your area of interest. But don't tear the material out and toss it in a box or drawer. Buy a box of manila folders when they are on sale, cut, date (date everything and note the source), and file it. When you start to write, you will have a file of valuable information at your fingertips.

I scan all my junk mail and have found some real treasures, quotes, suggestion, hints, and ideas that I have incorporated into my writing. Also, I always keep a notepad and pencil handy to jot down ideas, bits of conversation, and comments from teachers, children, and parents. The more organized your files and the greater amount of information you have on hand, the less research you will have to do when you begin writing.

Likewise, the more you know about publishing houses and what is and what isn't on the market, the easier it will be for you to sell your idea to a publisher.

Seminars and Workshops

Check with your local school district to find out about local, county, and state conferences, workshops, and seminars where educational materials are exhibited. Statewide teachers' unions have annual conventions and workshops, and science, math, and social studies associations sponsor workshops (see the appendix for a list of educational associations). At large events, you can spend several hours looking through and making notes on materials displayed. I have found that during the lunch hour the person in charge of the exhibit, who may be an editor or a marketing or sales representative, is not as busy and is often eager to talk about his or her line. Introduce yourself and mention your interest and the subject or title of the book you would like to write or the material you wish to develop. Ask for a business card and find out to whom you should send a query or proposal. Be sure to mention your conversation and when and where you met in your query letter. As in other fields, networking is important for writers specializing in education.

There is usually a fee for attending educational workshops and conferences; however, educational material exhibits are usually free and open to the public.

Publishers' Catalogs and Guidelines

Many educational publishers accept submissions from free-lance authors; some give assignments; others do all work in-house.

Most publishers, even smaller ones, if they accept free-lance material, have free authors' guidelines. Write for guidelines and be sure to include a self-addressed, stamped envelope (known everywhere as an SASE). Most publishers also offer free catalogs, though a few charge a small fee. When I write asking for guidelines, I also mention that I am enclosing a self-addressed mailing label (the adhesive-backed type) and, if available, would appreciate a copy of their current catalog. This is a fairly sure way of receiving a catalog quickly, as the label can be peeled off, attached to the catalog, and dropped in the outgoing mail. Otherwise, you will have to wait until someone gets around to typing a mailing label before the catalog can be sent.

When you receive the guidelines, read them carefully and study the publisher's needs so you will become familiar with the types of books or other educational materials they offer and the age or grade level for each. After learning about as many publishers and their materials as you can, make a list of possible publishers who produce material of the type you are considering.

Don't overlook infant/toddler and preschool materials! Both are growing markets. If you teach kindergarten or primary grades, you may eventually write a manual or resource book to introduce very young children to a particular curriculum area or to help in some way to prepare "little ones" for what lies ahead.

Do your homework. See if there is anything already available similar to what you wish to offer, how your idea differs, and what's unique about your own approach.

A publisher may be interested in single titles only; others consider series, and some accept proposals for both. Does your idea have series possibilities?

The appendix contains a comprehensive listing of publishers of educational materials and some of their needs; however, it is advisable to write for their guidelines and a catalog.

Personalized Market Charts

After making a list of companies you want to consider for your product, you may find it helpful to make a market chart of book publishers to whom you are particularly interested in submitting.

When I first started writing, I found my market chart to be an extremely helpful and time-saving tool. Study the sample chart and then make a similar one, personalizing it to fit your particular needs.

Once you branch out into the field, an additional chart for magazines and one for curriculum-related books (see examples) will save you valuable writing time searching lists for markets.

After making your chart, or from the market list in the appendix, list three or four possible markets for your material. Number

The Society for History Education

THE HISTORY TEACHER

Volume 25   Number 4   August 1992

*Published by the University Press at California State University,
Long Beach for the Society for History Education*

The History Teacher is published quarterly in November, February, May, and August of each year in affiliation with the American Historical Association and for members of the Society for History Education, C/o California State University, Long Beach, 1250 Bellflower Boulevard, Long Beach, CA 90840.

Membership dues: $22 for individuals; $15 for students with verification of enrollment; $28 for institutions. Foreign subscriptions: $32 for each membership category. All checks and money orders must be in U.S. dollars and drawn on a U.S. bank.

Single copies of the current issue and some copies of back issues since Volume 9 can be ordered from the Society for $8 per copy. All back issues are available on microfilm from University Microfilms, 300 N. Zeeb Road, Ann Arbor, MI 48106.

Returned or undeliverable copies of the journal and correspondence concerning subscriptions should be addressed to the Subscription Manager.

Notice of nonreceipt of an issue must be sent to the Subscription Manager within three months of publication of the issue. Changes of address should be sent to the Subscription Manager by the first of the month preceding the month of publication. The Society is not responsible for copies lost because of failure to report a change of address in time for mailing.

The Society cannot accommodate changes of address that are effective only for the summer months.

The History Teacher disclaims responsibility for statements, either of fact or opinion, made by contributors.

Second class postage paid at Long Beach, California, and at additional mailing offices. Publication number: ISSN 0018 2745; USPS number: 957:080; LC number: 74-3356.

Postmaster: Send change of address to The Society for History Education, California State University, Long Beach, 1250 Bellflower Boulevard, Long Beach, CA 90840.

The History Teacher publishes articles of three general types: (1) reports on promising new classroom techniques, educational programs, curricula, and methods of evaluating instructional effectiveness; (2) analyses of important interpretations, leading historians, historiographical problems, and recent trends in specific fields of historical research; and (3) critical review essays on audio-visual materials, textbooks, and other secondary works suitable for classroom use. Briefer items presenting ideas about teaching techniques, announcing conferences or workshops for history teachers, and the like, appear in the Society for History Education's newsletter, *Network News Exchange*, published each spring and fall as a part of *Perspectives*, a publication of the American Historical Association.

The History Teacher also publishes, as regular departments, reviews of audio-visual materials, textbooks, supplementary readers, and other printed classroom materials, with evaluations of their scholarly reliability, formats, and effectiveness of presentation. Reviews are commissioned in advance. Readers interested in contributing reviews should advise the Editor of their qualifications and fields of specialization.

The History Teacher does not have its own style sheet. Contributors should follow the forms of citation customary in the historical profession. Manuscripts must be double spaced (including all quotations and end notes), and submitted in triplicate. The manuscripts should be in letter quality type. Authors are encouraged to supply or recommend illustrations that would enhance the effectiveness of their work in print. Final decisions on manuscripts usually require a minimum of 10-15 weeks. We cannot return articles which have not been accepted unless a self-addressed, stamped envelope was enclosed with the article. The editors, who are the final judges of matters concerning grammar, usage, and other conventions, will edit contributions to conform to the normal manner of presentation in *The History Teacher*.

Manuscripts prepared on electronic word processing devices can dramatically improve the speed and accuracy of text handling. *The History Teacher* can accept many popular word processing formats. Contributors should indicate at the time of first (hardcopy) submission if their manuscripts are available in electronic form, identifying the word processing programs and the types of machine upon which the manuscripts were prepared. Upon acceptance, contributors will be informed if the manuscripts can be received in electronic form by *The History Teacher*.

Correspondence regarding contributions to *The History Teacher* and materials for review should be sent to the Editor, *The History Teacher*, California State University, Long Beach, 1250 Bellflower Boulevard, Long Beach, CA 90840.

The Society for History Education affirms that it does not discriminate on the basis of race, religion, national origin, age, or sex. Inquiries concerning the application of Title IX and other federal and state statutes may be referred to the Affirmative Action Officer, California State University, Long Beach, 1250 Bellflower Boulevard, Long Beach, CA 90840.

The History Teacher is abstracted or indexed in *Historical Abstracts, America: History and Life, Current Index to Journals in Education*, and *Multi-Media Index*.

Publishers since 1876

T.S. Denison and Company, Inc.

9601 Newton Avenue South • Minneapolis, MN 55431

Telephone (612) 888-1460

AUTHOR/MANUSCRIPT GUIDELINES

When submitting a manuscript for our evaluation, we suggest the following guidelines:

A. A manuscript should be neatly typed, double spaced, with 1-1/2 inch margins right and left, top and bottom.

B. Manuscript should have been proofread prior to submission.

C. Always have a copy (duplicate) of your manuscript. Frequently, manuscripts are lost or damaged in mailing.

D. Either by notation in the manuscript or on a separate sheet, list illustrations that are to appear in the published work.

E. Your manuscript should be checked and double-checked for accuracy and authenticity.

F. If permission is required to quote or utilize another source, secure these permissions and send with the manuscript. This should also apply to photos to be used from other sources.

G. We suggest that manuscripts be sent by UPS whenever possible. We have found this to be the safest and fastest manner of transporting them.

H. We prefer most of our manuscripts to conform to 32-48, 60 or 72 page books. There are exceptions, of course, but most of our materials will fit into this page format.

I. We will consider unsolicited manuscripts, and ask that return postage be included with such submissions.

Learning 93

AUTHOR GUIDELINES

Interested in writing for *Learning?* Then we're interested in you. Here's how to prepare and submit an article.

Preparing the article

What to write about: The article must be written for teachers of grades K-8. Our articles generally fall into three categories: how-to, why-to, and personal experience.

● How-to articles present techniques or materials that have proven effective in the classroom, and that readers can use in *their* classrooms.

● Why-to articles analyze and evaluate educational issues, theories, philosophies, trends — in a way that provides readers with new insight and understanding about how and why they teach.

● Personal experience articles tell either how you coped with a difficult person (student, parent, colleague, administrator), or how you overcame a situation that hampered your effectiveness as a teacher (curriculum constraints, unrealistic guidelines, difficult surroundings, and so forth).

How to write: To get a sense of the magazine's style, read recent issues of *Learning,* especially the articles similar to the kind you want to do. When you write:

● Avoid jargon.
● Use clear, simple language, and concrete examples and experiences.
● Make your point with specific information, not generalities.
● Write as if you were talking directly to the reader.

Submitting the article

The preferred length for *Learning* articles is 1500 to 3000 words. Your manuscript must be double-spaced and should be accompanied by a self-addressed stamped envelope so it can be returned if we decide not to publish it. If you wrote your manuscript on a computer, please indicate the computer and word-processing program you used. (Don't send a floppy disk.) Send the manuscript to: **Manuscript Submissions, Learning Magazine, 1111 Bethlehem Pike, P.O. Box 908, Springhouse, PA 19477.** We'll send an acknowledgment as soon as your manuscript arrives. A decision will take at least 4-8 weeks. If you want to enclose photographs, send prints, not negatives. Color or black-and-white are acceptable.

If it's accepted...

We pay between $50.00 and $300.00 for articles, depending on their length and quality. Payment is made on acceptance and gives us the exclusive right to publish your manuscript. Once your manuscript's been edited, we'll send you a copy for your inspection. Once it's been scheduled, we'll let you know the month. And, of course, once it's published, we'll send you a copy of the issue.

SPRINGHOUSE CORPORATION

1111 Bethlehem Pike • P.O. Box 908 • Springhouse, Pennsylvania 19477-0908 • (215) 646-8700

them in the priority by which you wish to submit. Then on the same day a manuscript is returned, you can readily check your markets, address your envelope, and mail it off the same day. If you want to sell, you have to have your manuscript or proposal off to a publisher.

Read, write, study, and become aware of the needs and gaps in the market for which you wish to write. The more you write, the better writer and the more professional you will become—and the more you will sell.

Resources for Market Guides

As an author or potential author, you will want to become familiar with as many resources as possible. Some educational publishers do not accept unsolicited manuscripts and therefore do not list in writers' guide books or periodicals. For addresses of resources listed below, and for a comprehensive market directory of educational publishers, see the appendix.

Teacher Aid/Resource Books

	Resource books	Patterns	Duplicating	Games	Task/flash cards	
Denison	√	√	√			
Fearon	√	√	√			
Good Apple	√	√	√	√	√	
Dale Seymour	√	√	√	√	√	

Curriculum-related Books

	Series	Biography	Science	Sports	History	
Facts on File	✓	✓	✓			
Millbrook	✓	✓	✓		✓	
Raintree	✓		✓	✓	✓	
Franklin Watts	✓	✓	✓		✓	

Literary Marketplace (LMP) is an oversized, annual publication listing national and international markets covering lists for literary agents, artists, and book reviewers. Also included are listings for book clubs, publishers, trade magazines, and news services.

The Writer's Handbook includes information on television scripts, popular verse, and markets for various types of literature.

Writer's Market is a hardcover market guide published annually in September. Among its market listings are books and magazines for both children and adults, screenwriting, and audiovisual materials. It contains only a limited number of listings for the educational market.

Children's Writer's & Illustrator's Market is a paperback juvenile market guide published annually in February. Among the markets covered are books, magazines, audiovisuals, and scriptwriting. It contains only a limited number of listings for the educational market.

The Writer is a monthly magazine for writers. The November issue contains an educational magazine market. Juvenile and teen-

Magazine Market Chart

	Fiction	Nonfiction	Puzzles	Crafts	Photos	
GENERAL						
Child Life	√	√		√	√	
Dolphin Log		√	√	√	√	
Highlights	√	√	√	√	√	
RELIGIOUS						
The Friend	√	√	√	√		
Noah's Ark	√	√		√	√	
Pockets	√	√		√	√	
EDUCATIONAL						
Learning		√	√			
Instructor Magazine		√	√		√	
Teaching/K–8		√	√		√	
Today's Catholic Teacher		√			√	

age magazine markets appear in April and family and parenting magazine markets in June.

Writer's Digest is a monthly magazine for writers. It offers a variety of magazine and book markets.

The above books can be ordered from the publisher, consulted at your local library, or purchased at bookstores.

El-Hi (elementary-high school), found in school textbook libraries and in some large public and college libraries, lists textbook markets.

The Children's Book Council's annual publisher's list of members is printed in February. The majority of the publishers are children's book publishers, but a few also publish curriculum-related books. The list is updated annually and is free for a first-class, self-addressed, stamped envelope.

The Society of Children's Book Writers and Illustrators makes a market list available at their annual August conference. It lists a few educational markets for supplemental books, but is available to members only.

Many other writing associations provide their members with various types of market lists.

Books in Print, found in the reference section of your library, lists all books in print in two separate volumes—under the author and title, or by subject, such as science, crafts, or ecology. There is also a supplement called *Forthcoming Books in Print.* By checking the subject volume, you can see how many books on your topic are in print, the copyright dates, publishers, and other information. Make yourself a copy of the pages that interest you to use for reference.

Although titles cannot be copyrighted, you can check under the author and title volume to see if there is another book with the title you have in mind. According to your contract, editors do have the right to change the title you have chosen. More about titles in chapter 4.

Published market lists are as current as possible. However, editors frequently move from one house to another, addresses do change, and companies are purchased by other companies. Unless you have a copy of recent guidelines from the publisher, it is usually wise to call the publishing company and ask the switchboard operator for the name of the editor to whom you should submit your query or proposal. Ask them to please spell the name. If gender is questionable, I always ask if it is Ms. or Mr.

3

Getting Your Ideas Together

"**W**HERE DO YOU GET YOUR IDEAS?" IS A FREQUENT question most authors are asked. For most published authors, whether for a picture book, novel, nonfiction, or some type of educational materials, ideas are never a problem. Once you write one book, you will discover there are dozens of books or products you would like to develop. As someone has said, "Ideas are a dime a dozen," and I agree. But it is what you do with your ideas and how you develop them in order to make a sellable book or product that is important.

As teachers and writers, you know that ideas are everywhere. Train yourself to be observant; take time to really look and listen and to make notes. You will find ideas at home, at school, at the market or mall, while visiting friends or relatives, while traveling, and in everything you do. Soon you will discover dozens of potential ideas worth pursuing. I now have more ideas in my files than I'll ever be able to develop even if I live to be a hundred. Although many of these ideas may not have the substance or the potential for a book or other project, they do provide me with a useful "bank" I can draw upon, and serve as springboards for further brainstorming.

How to Build an Idea Bank

The best way to start your own idea bank is to start an idea file. Making notes and clipping items from magazines, newspapers, or even junk mail (and a good filing system) can be tremendous motivators to start you writing. Often those flyers and letters you receive in the mail such as those advertising an ethnic cookbook, may start you thinking about a book on ethnic plays, or an article about easy recipes for celebrating cultural holidays for a teacher or children's magazine.

Collect all the information you can that has any relevance to your ideas and add it to your files. What's a good filing system? It's very simple: no computer hardware or software required; just treat yourself to a whole box of manila file folders, available from any office supply store. If they are on sale, buy two boxes. Label as many as you want, and start filling them with notes and clippings. You will discover that often one or two files will tend to generate many more. Here's an example: If you have more than one good idea, decide on the one that you are the most desirous of producing and concentrate on it. Maybe you have always wanted to write a craft book; however, you know there are many on the market. Science, too, is another strong interest, and you have always tried to make science more fun for your students by creating science-related puzzles and games. How about a science activity book that incorporates puzzles, games, and crafts, or maybe you feel there is enough material for two separate books? Start on the science book first, as you probably already have enough puzzle and game ideas to start writing your book proposal. Once the proposal is in the mail, start working on your ideas for the craft book. If stumped, ask yourself these ten questions:

1. Am I serious, as well as excited, about this project? Decide if this is something you have thought about for some time and not just an overnight "bright idea," and you feel strongly that it is something you must do.

Growth of an Idea Bank

Your first idea, or just one of several, evolves into many possibilities. What to put into your folders: items from magazines and newspapers, personal notes, sketches, charts, maps, outlines, names of resource people . . .

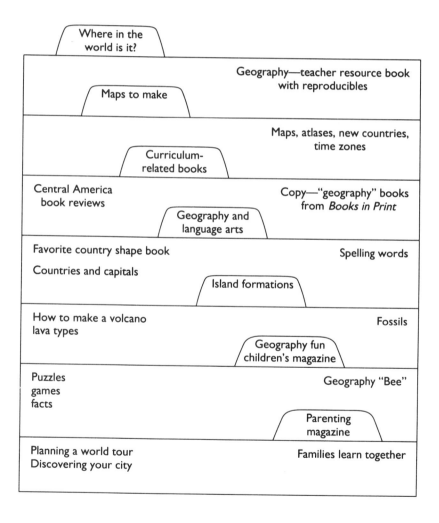

Where in the world is it?

Maps to make

Geography—teacher resource book with reproducibles

Curriculum-related books

Maps, atlases, new countries, time zones

Central America book reviews

Geography and language arts

Copy—"geography" books from *Books in Print*

Favorite country shape book

Countries and capitals

Island formations

Spelling words

How to make a volcano lava types

Geography fun children's magazine

Fossils

Puzzles
games
facts

Parenting magazine

Geography "Bee"

Planning a world tour
Discovering your city

Families learn together

2. Is it constantly on my mind? If the idea is continually on your mind, ideas keep popping into your head, and you keep making notes about the project and testing things out with your students, that's a good sign.

3. Is is topical, timely, and relevant? Talk with an education supply store manager, children's librarians, and other teachers about their opinions.

4. Is there enough material for a book, or is the product versatile? Could you come up with enough interesting information on your own, through research, and/or resource people to compile a book with a page count comparable to those you see in print?

5. Would teachers in more than one grade level be interested in this book or product? Maybe it could be used by all the lower primary grades, by after school programs, and for special education. If it is specifically for one grade, could you do a similar book for another grade or two?

6. Is it marketable? If you wish to sell the idea, you need to know the market. Would teacher supply stores, bookstores, and/ or retail stores buy it (ask the managers); and is it something you feel a publisher would be excited about or that would fit into their publishing lines?

7. Is there anything on the market that is similar? Probably, but maybe your idea is more advanced and would require students to use more reference materials such as an atlas or thesaurus.

8. Is it unique in some way? Maybe it has a new twist, such as a recently published counting book on counting backward.

9. If it is a game, learning toy, or other product, is it safe and durable, and can it be packaged? Make a list of what a child would learn from playing the game, and suggestions for eye-catching ways to package it—in a "shape" box, a colorful collage-decorated box, or a tall tube with a picture of the game board wrapped around the tube.

10. Am I willing to spend the necessary time required to develop this project? If you have a family, work full time, do volunteer work, play golf and tennis, and belong to several clubs, decide which activities you will happily give up to work on your idea. You need at least a year to devote to writing or developing the project.

If you answered yes to eight of the ten questions, you are ready to start writing, so write, write, write!

If you don't already have an idea but feel you would like to write for the educational market, the following will help you get started.

Make a list of five things you understand well enough to explain to teachers. For example, is spelling, art, or music one of your strong points and are you able to relate your interest to various areas of the curriculum?

Make a list of books or products you would buy if they were already on the market. Would you spend your own money to buy a book on multicultural approaches to teaching English, on storytelling for teachers and kids, or using fairy tales as the basis for a cross-curriculum approach to reading?

Make a list of ideas that have worked well in your own classroom such as the writing assignments you gave on "I am . . . (a historical figure)," writing about an object you draw from a paper bag, or on the first noun spoken to you when you get up in the morning.

Make a list of resources, supplements, visual aids, or related products that you have wished you had in your classroom but could never find. For example, a file on wheels where students could file their own work in folders during the week for take-home on Friday, or a guide to films, videos, and filmstrips on environmental topics with follow-up activities or projects.

When you decide on an idea, write down the competition you discovered while doing research on the markets. Editors are particularly interested in what is already on the market, and you can use this information in your query. Be sure to note the title, author, publisher or company, copyright date, price, and recommended age level.

Next write down the reason you want to write this book or develop this product.

Now describe your book or product in one sentence. This is a good opener for your proposal or query letter.

As you start to write, keep in mind that materials used in today's schools need to be representative of our multiethnic culture. Also be mindful of stereotyping or controversial topics (such as the paranormal, to name one example), as these may meet with negative reaction from some editors and educators.

While researching and writing, you will be surprised at the number of additional ideas that come to you. Write them down and put them in your files.

Keep a copy of all your research and correspondence, and date everything. It may not seem important at first, but once you start writing you will discover its value.

Sources

Magazines: I never read a magazine without having a pencil or marking pen handy. On the magazine's cover, I mark the page number of anything that interests me. Before the magazine is recycled, I can easily find the page and check to see if I want to keep it. If I feel it might be useful, I clip it or tear out the page, jot down the name of the magazine, issue date, and page number, and then file it in the appropriate file folder.

If I find something I want to keep in a magazine I read in someone's home or perhaps in the dentist's waiting room, I make a note of the title, issue date, and page number so I can check it out from the library and make a copy. After you get started on your project, many of the things you see, hear, and read will suddenly click and you will see it as an idea you may want to consider for the future. Be sure to make a note of it. Your notebook is as essential a tool as those file folders.

Newspapers: Not only do I clip from my daily newspapers but I also clip from those delivered to my hotel door when I am traveling. I do the same with advertisements, catalogs, and newsletters I receive. I seldom throw away any written material before I scan through it.

Another file I keep contains ethnic names. I have drawn from this file for one-page stories in workbooks, activity books, and for creating puzzles. A good source for names is telephone directories. When you visit a foreign country, take a few minutes to jot down names from the local telephone directory. Obituary columns, birth notices, and baby-name books will also provide you with a wide assortment of unusual names. Your name file can save you valuable research time later on.

A Place to Write

Many beginning writers feel, If I am going to write, I *need:*

A separate room for my office that will be used just for my writing. (Ideal, but *any* place can be a writing place. I read about a young mother who wrote her first book while standing at the fireplace mantel, sometimes holding a fussy baby in one arm, as she kept an eye on her busy toddler in the playpen.)

A large picture window that looks out into a colorful, inspiring garden. (Lovely, but good lighting and a potted African violet work just as well.)

A large, antique oak desk with plenty of drawer space and several four-drawer oak file cabinets to match my desk. (Nice; however, a kitchen table and a cardboard box with dividers and file folders have, in the beginning, worked well for many of us.)

A custom-made chair that fits every curve of my body and a matching chaise longue where I can be comfortable while outlining or editing. (Perfect, but a kitchen chair can give good back support, and any chair in the house or a seat on the subway works fine for editing.)

Bookshelves, floor to ceiling and the length of one wall, filled with reference books. (Fantastic, and you do need space for books; however, part of one shelf on the family bookshelf is a start, and your local library is filled with reference books.)

All of these "needs" sound great and they may be goals you will want to set for your ideal working environment, but don't use them for excuses for not writing. If you want to write, you will make the best of what is immediately available to you—just start writing!

A file cabinet is one of the best ways to organize your ideas, and I consider it to be one of an author's *first* investments. If you decide to purchase a file cabinet, plan ahead, for you will soon discover you never have enough file drawers. Eventually you may need a separate cabinet or drawer for ideas, projects you are working on, those you have off to publishers, and those you have sold.

Metal file cabinets come in several colors and have either two, three, or four drawers; wood cabinets usually have only two drawers as they are quite heavy, but they come with different finishes; and those made from heavy cardboard have one or two file drawers and are the least expensive. There are also portable file baskets on wheels that hold hanging files.

After a short period of trial and error, you will come up with your own filing system. You will find a set of alphabetical dividers to be a great help. Using a red felt marking pen, I label my individual folders in large letters.

Tools for Writing

Manuscripts written on a typewriter are acceptable by most publishers. A well-known, award-winning author I know has written over a hundred books on the typewriter. Either elite or pica type is acceptable; script and Old English typefaces are not. For all your correspondence and your final copy, you will want to use a new ribbon and make sure the print is clean and clear.

If you use a computer, remember that publishers will not accept dot matrix print. Letter quality or near letter quality is a necessity if you want your manuscript read. If you have a dot matrix printer, have your disk printed by a company that does letter-quality or laser printing.

If you are planning to buy a computer, talk with other writers and ask the salesperson for a demonstration before you buy. If you don't have a need for graphics or some of the other extra features of an expensive computer, look into a word processor such as Smith Corona or Brother. They sell for considerably less than a computer. Computers and word processors are certainly more efficient and time-saving. However, none of these, not even the most expensive, state-of-the-art ones, will make you a better writer. The act of writing itself makes you a better writer.

Publishers will not accept handwritten manuscripts no matter how legible your penmanship may be. However, if you don't type or own a computer, don't let that stop you! Write up your material and hire a professional typist to do the correspondence and final copy. Newspapers and the Yellow Pages list this service, but if you don't know the typist and his or her work, ask to see samples and for names of some current clients. Temporary employment agencies also provide people for typing services, but they are usually more expensive.

A recently published, thumb-indexed college dictionary with large print and a thesaurus are two other important tools for the writer. Even if these are built into your word processor, there will be times when you will want to check a written source. A set of encyclopedias, such as *World Book* is an excellent reference when writing materials to be used by children. Other references to consider are a rhyming dictionary, grammar book, Strunk and White's *The Elements of Style* (a small, inexpensive, yet valuable paperback), and *The Chicago Manual of Style*.

Gradually you will add to your collection of resources. If you can't find the information you need in your home resources, don't hesitate to contact the reference librarian at your public library or university. It is amazing what he or she can help you find.

You will want to be sure to save all your receipts when you buy reference books of any kind, for they, as well as any items you use for your writing, may be tax deductible.

Encyclopedias, dictionaries, reference books, writer's magazines, and other office "helps" are good items to put on your birthday or holiday "want list." I recently received two much appreciated gifts—an electric pencil sharpener and a postage scale—and now wonder how I ever managed without them.

The Writing Process

Step number one: Put it down on paper. Remember, you do not sell ideas that are only in your head. Start writing and don't worry about format, spelling, and punctuation—just keep writing.

You may wish to make a general outline, leaving plenty of space between chapters, and then go back and fill in more details.

Some people find writing on 3 × 5 index cards the way to start. The cards can then be shuffled around for placement and then numbered before they start typing.

You may be a writer who prefers to compose directly on a word processor or PC and then move the text around as you edit.

The way that works best for me is to write the chapter headings on separate sheets of paper and start writing with a pencil. I never erase, I just cross out, because I may want to use the material later. I leave a wide space between paragraphs and then cut the paragraphs apart. These are shuffled around, or laid out on a table, until I have the desired order. Then I number the pieces and clip the group together.

When I first start on a project, I use colored sheets of paper that I have saved from advertising and junk mail. Each chapter will have a different color. After folding the paper, I write the chapter number and title on the outside and slip any related material into it. As the work progresses, I transfer the colored papers to clearly labeled manila folders.

Scrap paper, cut into assorted sizes, makes handy note papers for jotting down thoughts, and they slip easily into your file. Both computers and typewriters generate an abundance of paper that can be recycled for this purpose as well as for outlining and making first drafts. But no matter what tool you use, the first step is the most important one: Get it down on paper. Write.

Audience Focus

Who will read your article? Who will buy your book? Consider the audience for whom you wish to write. Is it for the teacher's use, or for students, or both; for a specific age or grade level; or for more general use such as a pattern book? Most books usually do not cover a broad grade-level range. The generally accepted divisions are: preschool-kindergarten; kindergarten through third; fourth through sixth; upper and lower elementary or primary grades; middle grades or junior high; and high school or senior high.

Workbooks and worksheets are usually written for use with only one grade.

Format

You will want to think about the format of the book you wish to write before proposing it to a publisher, although the editor, packager, or publisher will make the final decision on format. Consider the following:

• What kind of a book will it be—resource or craft book, workbook, text, supplemental text, or a curriculum-related book?

• Will it need a teacher's or student's guide?

• How much information do I want to convey?

• What size do I visualize the book—for example, 8½ × 11 inches or 5 × 7 inches?

• How long should it be? If it has too many pages, it may be too expensive to produce or the size may make it difficult to handle. (Two separate books might be a possibility.)

• Will I need to include rough drawings or samples?

• Should it have a glossary, notes, or bibliography?

Now that you have your ideas together and you've organized your idea files and found a place to write, you are ready to start your query letter or proposal.

4

Selling Your Ideas

SELL BEFORE YOU WRITE (THE ADVICE IN THE PREVI-
ous chapter notwithstanding)! I sold, had the contract, and in
some cases received an advance before I wrote twenty-two of my
books. I don't mean I had not started on the books; I had prepared
a comprehensive outline and had already started a file for each
chapter.

You never want to send your complete manuscript unless the
publisher's guidelines require it, or until you are asked to do so.
If it is your first book or article, some editors may feel they need
to see your finished manuscript before they can make a decision.

Study the guidelines and send only what the editor requests,
such as a résumé, an outline or overview, and sample pages or
chapters. If they are interested, they will give you additional
guidelines. Also, they may like your idea but may wish to change
the format and age or grade level, or would like it written in a
different form.

I received my first book contract on the basis of a cover letter,
detailed outline, and four sample pages.

A well-known teacher-aid publishing company states their most common reasons for rejections are: (1) We already have a similar book; (2) the manuscript appears to be too short or is insubstantial in content; (3) the purpose of the proposed book and the audience are not well defined; (4) the logic of the arrangement (outline) is unclear.

Getting published, say experienced writers, results from knowing your audience, writing something meaningful to that audience, and writing it well.

Selecting Your Title

Some authors find naming their book or magazine article very difficult; others have so many titles they have trouble deciding on one.

If you can't come up with a title that pleases you, don't spend time worrying about it. Decide on an appropriate working title for your material and use it. Another title will no doubt come to you or your editor in the process of writing and researching.

On the other hand, you may have more than one good title and can't make a decision. Use one for your working title and mention the other one (no more than two) in your cover letter to the editor.

Selection of a title is important, for a title is what often motivates the editor to keep reading and it is important for marketing. A title for educational material needs to convey as clearly as possible the contents of the book. Titles for educational materials can be longer than picture books, novels, or nonfiction books. However, a short, catchy title may also be appropriate. In general, gimmicky or symbolic/poetic titles should be avoided. Titles should clearly communicate content.

My books, *Hats, Hats, and More Hats!* and *Is Your Storytale Dragging?* were both my original titles for two projects that were published, but *Science Toolbox: Making and Using the Tools of Science* was changed twice, and a pattern book went through five title changes and was changed from one large book to four small ones and back again to one book before it was published.

As an exercise, make a list of as many titles as you can think of.

Then choose the one that best represents the contents of your book. I read of one author who came up with fifteen titles for a book on pumpkin carving.

You might also consider a subtitle (explanatory title) as with this book, *How to Get Your Teaching Ideas Published* subtitled *A Writer's Guide to Educational Publishing*.

Remember, editors usually have the final say on a title, so don't be disappointed if they change yours, for their professional choices will sell more books. This applies as well to magazine articles.

Query

A query is a letter of inquiry to find out if a publishing house is interested in your idea. It usually contains the title of your proposed project, age range or grade level, and approximate word length, why it is different from others on the market, and your qualifications for writing the project. Some publishers wish to see a one- or two-page query. If they are interested they may send an author's questionnaire or project proposal form for more details on your project.

Book Proposal

Your proposal is an enlargement of your query. A cover letter, your résumé, table of contents, an outline, and sample activity pages or chapters are included with your proposal.

Cover Letter

Your cover letter is an important element in your presentation. Try to keep it to one page or no more than a page and a half. It should state what research you have done to determine why your project should be published; what projects similar in nature are on the market; how your project differs; what yours can do that is better, more useful, and unique.

Acknowledging the competition and providing detailed information about competing books takes time and work, but clearly indicates you have done your homework; it also helps the editor make a decision about your proposal.

If you have any publishing credits or can help promote your product, mention this in your cover letter.

(Date)

Senior Editor
Franklin Watts, Inc.
387 Park Avenue South
New York, NY 10016

Dear Senior Editor:

I would like to present a proposal for a nonfiction book, *Crystals and Crystal Gardens You Can Grow.*

This book presents easy-to-understand information on crystals: how they are formed, and where they can be found. Directions for "growing" twelve different kinds of crystals and crystal gardens, each with its own unique formation, a recipe for a simple, basic solution, and a listing of easy to obtain items and materials are included.

The experiments are easy and safe enough for children to do on their own. However, teachers, youth leaders, and librarians will also find them to be a welcome addition to their programs.

These interesting projects will motivate young scientists to observe, experiment, and make discoveries. In most instances, change and "growth" take place quickly, giving instant feedback and reinforcement to the experimenter.

According to my research, there is no recent book on this subject. Neither is there a book in print that offers such a wide collection of recipes for crystals while providing the reader with interesting background information on crystals and their formation.

My credits include twelve published books and over one hundred magazine items. My background includes teaching kindergarten through third grade, ten years at the community college teaching science to student teachers, science classes for the University of California Extension at Santa Barbara, California, and conducting science enrichment classes for upper elementary students.

An outline, Part II, Part III, and a self-addressed, stamped envelope are enclosed. This is *not* a multiple submission.

Your consideration of my proposal will be appreciated.

Sincerely,

Jean Stangl
(Address)
(Telephone number)

(Date)

Articles Editor
The Dolphin Log
8440 Santa Monica Boulevard
Los Angeles, CA 90069

Dear Articles Editor:

Are iceworms for real? Yes, they are! On a recent trip to Alaska, I discovered these interesting little creatures living between ice crystals near the surface of a glacier. I also talked with one of the rangers at Portage Lake where I was able to observe these tiny animals with a hand lens as they wiggled in, out, and across a chunk of ice. I was fascinated!

Upon my return home, I decided to do some research. I would like to share my experience and research with your readers via my article "Who Ever Heard of Iceworms?"

My credits include twenty-two published books and over two hundred magazine items.

A self-addressed, stamped envelope is enclosed for your reply.

Sincerely,

Jean Stangl
(Address)
(Telephone number)

(Date)

Acquisitions Editor
Murphy's Video Productions
1841 Brookline Drive
Denver, CO 80218

Dear Acquisitions Editor:

School bus safety is everyone's business! With so many students riding school buses across our nation today, everyone—students, bus drivers, teachers, and parents—needs to be made aware of the importance of bus safety.

At the request of our school district, I have worked out a script for a school bus safety video. "Barney Bear Rides the Bus" consists of live action showing children entering and leaving the bus exercising safety, and an animated Barney Bear superimposed on each frame. The video runs approximately ten minutes.

I have produced videos for the college where I work part time in the audiovisual department and am interested in either providing the script or producing the entire video. Enclosed is a list of the educational videos I have written and/or produced.

Would you be interested in seeing the script for "Barney Bear Rides the Bus" and a copy of one of the videos I have produced?

A self-addressed, stamped envelope is enclosed for your reply.
I look forward to hearing from you.

Sincerely,

Jean Stangl
(Address)
(Telephone number)

If you are qualified and wish to do your own illustrations, mention this in your cover letter. Don't send any samples of your art unless they are essential to or would enhance your proposal. Never send originals of drawings; send photocopies only. Sell the publisher your book idea first. The editor will then tell you what he or she would like to see for art evaluation.

Professionalism is important. Use a business letter format and always enclose a self-addressed, stamped envelope for the return of your proposal or an answer to your query letter.

Résumé

A résumé—also known as "CV," curriculum vitae or vita—is a *short* account of one's career and qualifications. You don't want to bore the reader with your life history, so make your résumé short, easy to read, and as interesting as possible. An editor wants someone who can create interesting materials. Your résumé should demonstrate that your background and experience dovetails with the proposed project and that you understand the professional requirements for a successful product.

A college transcript is not a substitute for a résumé; neither is a diploma or certificate. If you do not already have a current résumé, write one! Make yourself several copies to have available. Books on how to write a good résumé are available at your local library.

Some publishing houses ask for a bio or biographical sketch, which is similar to a résumé, submitted in addition to it. Your bio should also include any publishing credits. Tip: Look at the author bios on book jackets, then write one about yourself. Limit it to *one* paragraph.

Even if the editor is not interested or cannot use your proposed idea at the time, your writing skills and résumé may be impressive and they may be kept on file for other projects that come up. This can—and often does—result in a future assignment.

Table of Contents

When writing your table of contents make sure each chapter title clearly and concisely tells what you expect to include in that chapter, and that a quick reading of the chapter titles will give a good overall picture of the proposed book. The table of contents should also back up the title you have chosen. It may help to have subsection titles to tell more about each chapter. This is especially important if you are not including a detailed outline or sample pages.

Outlines

A good idea is not enough. You must write a detailed outline that gives a description and overview of your product.

Under each chapter heading you may wish to write a descriptive paragraph of what you plan to include, or you can use a standard outline and break it down into levels and sublevels.

Once you have established a good working relationship with an editor, your proposals won't need to be so detailed. I sent five ideas, consisting of two short paragraphs each, for teacher resource books to an editor I had been working with. She was interested in three of them and after sending the requested outline and table of contents, I received my contracts.

Introduction

The introduction should tell why you are writing the book and for whom. Try to limit it to one page. When you write the actual book, you can add to it. Editors like an intriguing introduction, and it helps sell your idea. Readers prefer short introductions that lure them into the book so they can discover new ideas, unique projects, and innovative aids for teachers.

Try writing a catalog blurb for your book. This exercise will force you to identify two or three strong selling points and to phrase them in a way designed to grab the attention of a potential buyer. Incorporate all or as much as is appropriate into your introduction.

Using the one sentence you came up with in chapter 3 to describe your book makes an enticing first sentence for your introduction.

Sample Pages

Whether you need to include sample pages will depend on the type of book you are proposing. A book of worksheets, patterns, puzzles, or science or math lab-type reproducibles would necessitate doing so.

For my book on making hats, I enclosed several sample pages with rough drawings and directions, and I also made two sample paper hats. With *Paper Stories,* it was necessary to include three or four sample outline patterns as well as the finished visual aid, as the patterns are cut as the story is read and each surprise ending depends on seeing the cut-out.

If you feel sample pages are necessary for clarification, then include them in your package.

Proposing a Book Series

You may feel your book has potential for a series of books; if so, mention this in your cover letter. If it is a unique workbook that could become a set of three books for each of three grade levels, or the same slant could be used for different areas of the curriculum and you feel you can do the project, then by all means, suggest it to the editor.

I sold my proposal for a series of three books, *Magic Mixtures,*

Flannelgraphs, and *Fingerlings,* using the subtitle "Fun for Little Ones." Since each book was of an entirely different category, I wrote three separate outlines.

A recent publisher's catalog lists a series of independent activity books in which one author wrote similar books for each grade, one through six, with the same illustrations on the cover. Another catalog lists two separate authors writing similar books titled *Book I* and *Book II.*

A publisher may have an existing series, and you may feel you have a good idea for another book to add to the series (if you note in the publisher's catalog that different authors were used). You will want to read as many books in the series as possible, even if you have to buy copies. Consistency is important in series books in the number of pages, size of the book, and the way material is presented. Remember it is the editor's series and you must write to the existing format.

How Long Until You Hear It's a "Go"?

Keep in mind that the first thing your publisher reads is the title, then the table of contents, outline, and the introduction, if it is included. Make your introductory package one that the editor can't resist. Be sure to provide sufficient postage on both the proposal and the enclosed self-addressed, stamped envelope. Keep in mind that the material must sell itself; you won't be able to accompany your proposal to explain or amplify its merits.

Waiting for a response from an editor always seems to the author to take too long. Some publishers respond to a query or proposal in six weeks, others take three to six months. Your editor may be interested, but it may be standard practice to send proposals to an outside reader who is an expert in that particular field for comments. If your proposal is returned, you may receive a copy of the comments. If so, you will want to study them carefully and perhaps make some changes in your proposal before you send it out again.

Multiple Submissions

This is a much debated subject. Multiple submissions, also called simultaneous submissions, means making copies and sending them to several different publishers at the same time. Most editors don't like them but expect to be informed if they receive one; others will not accept them. Authors, especially first-time authors, feel it is unfair to have to wait so long for a decision. Usually editors do not mind if you send multiple, one-page query letters. But when you send a proposal and include sample chapters, this requires time to read, evaluate, and come to a decision. Multiple submitting is a decision authors must make for themselves. However, if you decide to take this approach, be prepared to deal with the situation should two or more editors wish to offer you a contract based on your proposal.

Rejections

Regardless of how many books or articles one has sold or how many rejection letters one receives, a rejection letter is not easy to accept. However, we all get them. Two authors I know, who have each written over a hundred books, say they still get rejection letters.

Try to think of rejection letters as I do—"those little pieces of paper that come with my returned manuscript"—and send your material off to the next publisher on your list. You are not being rejected and neither is your manuscript. In most cases, as the note says, it is not right at this time for this publisher's needs, so keep sending your proposal. Typical rejection letters consist of one page, a half page, a strip of paper, or a postcard—I have received many of each. Usually they are not signed or dated (date it before you file it) and are form letters. However, an editor may add a handwritten note to the form rejection such as: we like your style, we have something similar in the works, or try us again. This is a good sign and you should feel encouraged, because you are on the right track.

I had one proposal rejected by a publisher who, after two years, when I sent it to him again, sent me a contract within a week.

Look at rejection slips as a part of the business of writing. Here is a classic rejection letter that has been around for some time and no one seems to know with whom it originated. I have heard it referred to as a "Chinese rejection letter," and one publication said it actually appeared in an economic journal. Here is one of the many versions I share with my writing students. "We have read your manuscript with boundless delight. If we were to publish your paper it would be impossible for us to publish any work of a lower standard. And as it is unthinkable that, in the next thousand years, we shall see its equal, we are, to our regret, compelled to return your divine manuscript, and to beg you to overlook our short sight."

It is well to remember that publishing companies and manufacturers receive hundreds of inquiries from prospective authors. In order to ensure that yours will receive careful consideration, be sure it is neat, well written, concise, and descriptive.

By the time you prepare and mail your first proposal, you no doubt have come up with one or a dozen other viable ideas that you can't wait to start. Do it—start working on your next proposal *now*.

A few further words about that magazine article you want to write . . .

A query is usually sent for parenting, teacher, and children's nonfiction articles. It is usually only one page and provides an overview of the article you are proposing. It should include (1) What your article is about (one or two sentences to grab the editor's interest); (2) length (page or word), or category (for the Teacher Express column, Parenting News or First Person Experiences column); (3) your qualifications for writing the article (you are a media specialist, teach classes for exceptional children, you lead summer nature hikes for kids and parents); (4) an outline or a one- or two-paragraph overview.

The samples on pages 37–40 showed a query for a book, magazine article, and a product. Chapters 13 through 16 cover different categories within the magazine market.

5

Illustrations and Artwork

ILLUSTRATIONS ADD TO THE ATTRACTIVENESS, READ-ability, and sellability of a book and can be used effectively to break up the text. In educational materials, art can and should reinforce and amplify the text. A combined visual/verbal approach is essential in presenting many concepts—pictures and words work together in effective teaching. Even if your own art background is minimal, you can use art as a tool to help bring your writing ideas to life. Keep in mind that illustrations should help in the teaching process; do not use them simply as decorations.

Some publishers use illustrations more freely than others. Workbooks, worksheets, reproducibles, and pattern books naturally require art. Learning games and toys often contain illustrated rules, guidelines, or direction sheets.

Illustrations should not be sent with your query letter, except for worksheets, patterns, and similar pages that make up the proposed book.

If, like many educational material writers, you are not artistic, rough drawings, bubbles containing a description of the art, stick figures, or whatever you can provide to clarify your idea are acceptable.

Responsibility for Artwork

Writers ask, "Am I responsible for the artwork?" Usually illustrations for books are taken care of by the publishing house. You are responsible only for the text. If there is no reason you need to review the artwork, you may not see the illustrations or drawings until you receive a copy of the book. But don't be alarmed, the finished book is usually far beyond your expectations.

However, some companies may send you several pieces of rough artwork as a courtesy, or you may be sent drawings to check for accuracy for experiments or construction projects, or for a craft or how-to book. In a book contract, this may be a negotiable issue.

Large publishers have in-house illustrators who will work with your editor, others send the work out to free-lance illustrators.

Some companies do expect the author to furnish finished art. If you are not an artist, you will need to hire someone to make drawings or whatever is needed.

If you do not know a professional artist you may be able to locate one through a college or university art department, the Yellow Pages, advertising agencies, or through a graphics print shop. Check out their work first and make sure they can supply what your editor requires. Ask to see their portfolio or samples of published art. If you are pleased, have them make a few sample drawings that represent your book, which you can send to the editor for approval before committing yourself to the artist.

Also make sure you have a contract for your book before you engage an illustrator. You will need a written agreement stating the number of illustrations needed, deadline, price and when it is to be paid, and assurance the art will be redrawn until it meets the approval of your editor. Cover all facets, because you are the person responsible for providing the camera-ready art for your book. It is important to have the agreement in writing and to have it signed, dated, and notarized.

Most magazines contain illustrations or artwork, but again the author does not have to supply the illustrations, except perhaps to show a pattern, puzzle grid, or craft project. The publisher provides the necessary artwork or illustrations; however, if you are a professional illustrator, many publishers welcome a package of manuscript and artwork.

Author-Illustrator Duo

Working with an illustrator friend or relative for a year or so to develop a finished book often is not a wise undertaking. Illustrations should come after the book has been sold.

Give careful thought to the pros and cons of working with an artist, no matter how good a friend, *before* you agree to split the royalties when you sell the book. You may sell your book idea, but the editor may not feel the illustrations or drawings are of professional quality.

After receiving your contract, which might call for you to supply the finished art, you can send in a few of your friend's samples, prepared for your book, for approval. After acceptance, *then* decide (1) if you want to pay your friend outright for doing the art (work for hire); (2) if you are going to share the royalties based on a contract between the two of you; (3) whether to make the artist a party to the publisher's contract. If you buy the drawings, will the artist's name appear on the inside or cover of the book? Regardless of your decision, work up an agreement form as mentioned. This is necessary even if the illustrator is your spouse, friend, or relative.

If you, as the artist, are working together with the author on a project such as a pattern, bulletin board, or craft book and your work has been accepted by the editor, you each may be issued separate contracts and share equally in the royalties and advance if one is given.

Illustrating Your Own Work

Publishers welcome authors who are also illustrators and wish to do their own art. If no illustrations are necessary for your book, you may still wish to do some art to enliven it. If so, mention this in your cover letter. If interested, the editor will tell you what kind of samples to send for consideration.

A publisher may have specific guidelines or a manual that covers artwork. Your contract sometimes tells you the number of illustrations or drawings planned for your book.

Most of the artwork in educational material consists of black-and-white line drawings, which are easy to print or reproduce. Except for the cover or book jacket very little color art is used. However, nonfiction, picture, and curriculum-related books for very young children will require, in most cases, color illustrations.

Illustrators are given freedom to add illustrations for aesthetic and pleasing value in some types of books, but the artist is more limited in educational materials such as workbooks and teacher resource books.

A helpful brochure for illustrators on showing your artwork is available for an SASE and one dollar from Children's Book Council, 568 Broadway, New York, NY 10012. Ask for their guide on illustrating children's books.

The Society of Illustrators and the Graphic Artists Guild will send you information on their professional organizations.

The Graphic Artists Guild recommends two books, both published by Haworth (which are available from the guild): *The Business of Being an Artist* and *How to Sell Your Photographs and Illustrations.*

For addresses, see the appendix.

Computer-generated Art

A new entry in publishing is the use of interactive media, using CD ROM players and similar technology. Printed-page books will be with us for many years to come; they will simply have to share the market with new, emerging technology. However, these new teaching methods still begin with the written word and a pencil sketch for art.

Being computer literate is essential for both the writer and illustrator of educational material. The School of Visual Arts in New

York City now offers a degree in computer illustration. Writers and artists should check out courses offered by accredited schools. Nearly all teach state-of-the-art courses in their evening or continuing education programs. Schools with good programs include Chicago Art Institute, Otis in Los Angeles, California Institute of the Arts, Parsons and Pratt in New York City, and the Rhode Island School of Design.

What kind of a computer should one buy? The best place to start is to talk to other illustrators who use this technology and with publishing houses you wish to contact for assignments. If you are in the market for a computer, look for one that will be compatible with your publishing house.

In software, you will need top page layouts and illustration programs, and, if you can afford it, a laser printer and a color monitor with a full-page view. Scanners are used by both illustrators and designers. Illustrators need them for scanning their pencil sketches for use with their illustration pages, and designers use them for scanning photos and line art for inclusion in their pages.

Selling Your Artwork

If you are interested in illustrating educational materials but do not wish to submit a book idea for consideration, send an in-depth query describing the kind of work you do, a résumé, your availability, computer skills, and photocopies of some of your work (three or four copies of work that is current). Ask if you can present a portfolio (either by mail or in person) and what they would like included. You can submit this material to several publishers for whom you would like to work.

A portfolio contains a more extensive view of your abilities such as completed books, mounted pages of art or a page design, original art, and transparencies of art. Major art schools offer workshops in portfolio preparation.

You may also wish to contact a publishing company by phone. Ask the switchboard operator whether you should speak to the editorial director or the art director. If the company is nearby, you may be able to make an appointment to show your portfolio; if not, find out what you need to send. Always record the date of all phone calls and the person's name.

When sending artwork, make certain each piece is properly identified and that each contains your name, address, and telephone number. Include a short cover letter directed to the person you have been in contact with, mentioning either the date of the phone call and what was discussed, or the response to your query letter. Suggestions for mailing a portfolio are given under "Mailing Artwork and Photographs" in this chapter.

Educational publishers and book publishers are not the only ones who need illustrators. Both educational and children's magazines, religious material and magazines, and newsletter publishers all require the services of an illustrator. Covers and jackets for books, and boxes for games, toys, manipulatives, and puzzles also use illustrators.

Photographs

A rubber stamp or an adhesive-backed label with your name, address, and telephone number is a good way to identify photographs.

Black-and-white glossy prints or 35-mm colored slides, also called transparencies, are commonly used in books and magazines. Most magazines and book publishers require a model/property release.

If you are doing a nonfiction photo-essay book or one containing photographs, you need to be able to provide the photos. If you cannot take professional photographs yourself, but need to supervise the photography, you will have to hire someone to take them. Your publisher may provide an advance toward the cost, with the average being $250 to $1,000.

Many types of photographs are available free or can be purchased from photo stock houses. Some free sources are the U.S. Department of Agriculture for pictures of food and flowers; travel agencies or airline companies for countries, people, industry, buildings, and places of interest; chambers of commerce for historical houses, celebrity homes, monuments, museums, and other places of interest. The Library of Congress, state and national archives, and state libraries supply photographs and slides for a copying fee. Most newspapers charge a fee for use of their photographs.

Some sources for slides and photographs are the Encyclopedia of Associations, which lists names and addresses of manufacturers and associations and U.S. chambers of commerce. Addresses for all embassies can be found in the reference section of most libraries. Write or call for photo information. Library of Congress, Photo Duplication Service, Washington, DC 20540; NASA Photographic Index, Public Affairs Division—LFD-2, Washington, DC 20546; Photography Division, Office of Government & Public Affairs, U.S. Department of Agriculture, Washington, DC 20250 (ask for "Guide to USDA Photos"); and Photographic Library, U.S. Department of the Interior, National Parks Service, P.O. Box 37127, Washington, DC 20013–7127 are all possible sources for free photographs and transparencies. If you cannot find what you need, check the Yellow Pages of large city telephone directories (found in most libraries) for photo stock houses.

Whether using free photographs or ones you've paid for, a credit line should be given, usually on the copyright page of a book or under or next to the photo in a magazine. You will need to write captions for all photographs you submit. Always include credit lines with captions. Don't overlook the courtesy of sending a thank-you note for use of free photographs, and if it is for a magazine, send along a tear sheet or photocopy of the article.

Publishing houses sometimes take on the responsibility of providing photographs for your book. For a book I wrote on crystals, my editor selected the color photographs from photo sources, provided an illustrator for the line drawings, and still gave me the full royalty and advance.

With another publishing house, I was invited to send a color photograph for consideration for the cover.

Magazine guidelines usually specify black-and-white glossy prints for inside. A 9 × 12 print is the preferred size, as they are easier to work with and can be reduced without distortion. Color photographs are most frequently used on the cover. You should never send negatives unless they are requested. Also, you should not send photos with your magazine manuscript, but mention their availability in your cover letter.

Color photographs are used in many children's, religious, and educational magazines, and the photo needs are generally listed in the magazine's guidelines.

Additional resources for illustrators and photographers can be found in the appendix.

Mailing Artwork and Photographs

For assembling your manuscript/art/photo package, follow the publisher's guidelines. For a book, the art, along with a figure caption list, is usually packaged separate from the manuscript. With workbooks and craft books, the art pages may be numbered along with the text.

Send your prints in photo mailers and transparencies in protective sleeves, and mail them Federal Express or some other way by which they can be tracked if necessary.

Artwork, depending on the amount, can either be packaged with the manuscript or sent in a separate package (be sure to include a cover letter). Use sturdy boxes and tape it securely.

When mailing a portfolio, be sure to package it carefully. You may want to send it Priority Mail or UPS (United Parcel Service). It is a good idea to send all artwork by registered or certified mail with a return receipt requested.

Payment for Artwork

Payment for books is usually set by the publishers or determined after the designer has figured out the page price. But you should be prepared to price your job or your services should you get an acceptance from the publisher.

Fees vary according to the type of book.

Nonfiction and curriculum-related books
  Cover or jacket—$500 to $1,000
  Cover and interior illustrations—$2,000 to $3,000

Workbooks, craft, and resource books
 Cover—$200 to $300
 Interior:
    color—$60 to $75 per page
    line drawings—$30 to $40 per page

Magazines often pay for the package, manuscript and illustrations. The more popular and well-known magazines pay the highest rates; the pay scale for religious magazines, both educational and for children, may be slightly lower. Payment varies considerably as each magazine is different, consequently many factors determine the payment. Therefore, it is always best to check the magazine's guidelines for needs and payment.

Children's magazines
 B/W, inside—$10 to $100
 Color, inside—$50 to $300
 Cover, color—$75 to $750

Educational magazines
 B/W, inside $15 to $50
 Color, inside—$50 to $100
 Cover, color—$100 to $300

Payment for Photographs

Nonfiction, photo-essay, and picture books usually pay 8 to 10 percent royalty with an advance of $500 to $3,000, if you provide the photographs. If a photographer works with you on a book and provides the photos, you split the advance and royalty fifty/fifty.

Magazines often pay by the package—manuscript and photographs. The pay scale for religious magazines, both educational and for children, may be slightly lower. The more popular and well-known magazines pay the highest rates.

Children's magazines
 B/W, inside—$25 to $500, or $100 to $500 per project
 Color, inside—$150 to $800

B/W, cover—$35 to $250
Color, cover—$50 to $1,000

Educational magazines
B/W, inside—$15 to $110
Color, inside—$50 to $200
Cover, color—$100 to $300

6

The Writing Business

ONCE YOU START WRITING FOR PUBLICATION, YOUR writing becomes a business. The more you understand about different aspects of writing as a business, the better your chances are of being successful.

It's unlikely that you will become rich from your royalties on the first books you write, even if you have several successful books on the market that will pay you good royalties. It is not even realistic to think that several books will put you in a high-income bracket. However, if you have steady book contracts, write for several publishing companies, and are willing to take on a variety of assignments, you can make a good living writing in this field.

Writing magazine articles often is more lucrative than books, but having a book published often provides an entrée to getting more magazine and journal articles published. There's a monetary synergy among media.

Another way authors of educational material supplement their writing income is by teaching classes on writing, by presenting seminars and workshops, and by speaking at conferences on topics based on their books and articles.

However, if you are employed, it is not advisable to give up your job until you are established as a writer. Don't quit teaching! Writing and teaching are synergistic professions; one stimulates the other.

Contracts

A contract is a written, legal agreement between the publishing company and the author defining the responsibilities of each.

Upon the decision of the publisher to accept your proposal package, you will receive either a telephone call from the editor or a letter stating briefly the terms, advance, royalty, and due date. In smaller companies, your editor may also be the publisher and even own the company.

When the editor receives your oral or written agreement, the contract will usually follow within the next two or three weeks. Usually you will receive two copies to sign and return. The publisher then signs and returns a copy to you. Before you sign, you will want to read the contract through to make sure you understand the terms.

The so-called standard form contract is used by many publishers. Although they may contain similar information, each is individualized for that particular publishing house. A contract may be from one to eight pages long. As a teacher, you are certainly capable of reading and understanding your contract. You do not need a lawyer, because in some cases you may know more about writing and contract terms than your attorney, unless, of course, you are dealing with an attorney who specializes in book contracts. If there is any part of the contract you do not understand, do not hesitate to call your editor and ask for clarification.

If your contract is for a series, one contract may cover all books in the series, but the titles will be listed separately and the length of time for the completion date will be totaled.

If you are cowriting, both authors' names will appear on the same contract with author copies provided for both.

Your reference librarian can help you locate a sample, standard book contract or you may find one in a how-to book on writing.

Publisher's Responsibility

Your contract will define both the publisher's and the author's responsibilities. Basically it states that on a royalty contract, the publisher will

- Publish the book.
- Pay the author an advance of a certain amount.
- Pay the author a royalty percentage at a specified period.
- Copyright the book.
- Market the book.
- Send author's copies to author.
- Return all rights to the author if the book goes out of print.

Author's Responsibility

As the author, your obligation is to

- Deliver the final manuscript acceptable to the publisher on or before the date stated in the contract.
- Submit the manuscript on disk, and illustrations, if required.
- Meet the required word or page length.
- Provide permission forms if using copyrighted material in any form.
- Revise and rewrite if necessary.
- Abide by the option clause.

Rights

Your contract will inform you of all the rights you have under the contract, such as foreign or translation rights; serial; book club, audio, and video rights. Royalty-paying companies usually provide additional payment to the author for most subsidiary rights.

Some publishers have their own book clubs; others presell to book clubs either as a premium for new book club members, or as a monthly selection. Newbridge (formally Macmillan), Library of Special Education, and Instructor (Scholastic) Book Clubs all offer educational materials to book club members.

Magazine rights are discussed in chapter 13.

Royalties and Advances

Royalties are usually paid annually, although a few companies pay semiannually. Except in the case of smaller companies, you will usually receive a royalty statement at the end of the royalty period, which is stated in your contract. It also tells you that the check itself will be mailed two months or so later.

Royalty payments vary considerably depending on the type of book, grade level, and length, but on the average here is the range you can expect:

Educational resource books, 3 to 10 percent
Workbooks, 3 to 5 percent
Curriculum-related books, 8 to 10 percent
Elementary and secondary texts, 4 to 10 percent
College texts, 12 to 20 percent
Book club sales, usually one-half the regular royalty

If you are cowriting, you will share the royalty with your coauthor. If you are a contributor to a text, it may be a shared royalty or a flat fee depending on your contribution and the type of book and grade level.

Royalties may be paid either on the wholesale (net cash or net sales) or retail list price. Retail stores usually receive a 40 percent discount, so royalty income is often based on the discount price rather than the price printed on the book jacket.

If you sell your book outright (for a flat fee), the range may be from $200 to $6,000 depending on the type of book and grade level.

Your contract may contain an escalating clause, or sliding scale, which means that after a certain number of books are sold over the first printing, the royalty percentage will increase. This is a common practice especially for smaller publishers. The theory behind this arrangement is that the publisher has a better chance to recover costs early on, and when the book proves itself by continued sales and popularity, the author gets a larger share.

Also, after you have written two or more books for the company, they may raise the percentage, or you may be able to negotiate for either a larger percentage or advance.

Advances also vary and depend upon the type of book and whether this is your first book. Advances can run from $300 to $5,000 for books. Remember that an advance is not an outright gift, but an advance against your first royalties, and it will be deducted from your first royalty check. Some publishers offer half of the advance upon signing the contract and the other half after the complete manuscript has been accepted, or upon actual publication of the book.

Not all educational publishers give advances. However, when you do receive an advance against royalties, you can be fairly certain your book will be published. If no advance is given and no publication date is listed in the contract, there is a chance your book will not be published or a least not within a reasonable length of time. Any number of events might be the reason for a long delay or postponement. Editors do leave companies for various reasons and move from publishing house to publishing house, and companies are often purchased by another company that moves it to another state, or the company goes into bankruptcy.

I had one of these situations happen with three books I had written under contract to add to an existing series. Several changes took place within the organization, and after three years, two of my books had not been published. Since the company could not promise when they would be published, I was offered a cash settlement, which I accepted. They returned all rights to me and I was able to offer the manuscripts to another company.

Work for Hire

If you sell your book to the publisher on a work for hire basis, also called flat fee or outright purchase, you relinquish all rights. Your book is copyrighted in the publisher's name and you receive no royalties. However, your name usually appears on the cover.

One of the advantages of accepting this one-time payment is that it comes to you upon completion of your manuscript, whereas with a royalty contract, if you do not receive an advance, it may be two years after finishing the manuscript before you receive your first royalty check.

An average range for work for hire payments is:

Resource and workbooks—$200 to $600
Worksheets—$20 to $50
A chapter for an upper elementary math book—$400 to $1,000
Textbook chapter (K–6)—$500 to $2,000
Activity sheets—$15 to $60

Copyright

If you would like information on the copyright law, you can write to the Register of Copyrights, U.S. Copyright Office, Library of Congress, Washington, DC 20559. There is no charge for the copyright handbook.

Under the copyright law your writing is protected from the time you put it on paper, because the law recognizes the creator of the work as the owner. Because your work is automatically copyrighted at the time of origin, there is no need to apply for a registered copyright if you plan to submit your work to a publisher. Most publishers are reluctant to deal with previously copyrighted material, and submitting it this way may label you as an amateur.

If you are the sole author and you sold your book on a royalty basis, your book will be copyrighted by the publisher either in your name or the publisher's name (as stated in your contract). Educational material is often copyrighted in the publisher's name. Some textbooks and most curriculum-related books are copyrighted in the author's name. Your publisher is responsible for sending in the two copies required by the copyright office and paying the copyright fee.

Illustrations can also be copyrighted. See chapter 5.

In some cases, there may be a need to copyright nonbook materials (see chapter 9).

Option Clause

Your contract may contain an option clause that states that the publishing house has an option on your next book, providing it is the type of book they buy. Also, a time limit is specified for giving you a decision on your next proposal. If they turn it down, you are free to submit to another publisher. Often the option clause is a negotiable issue, depending on the nature of your project—fiction versus nonfiction, for example.

Out of Print

As long as your book continues to sell, your publisher will keep printing it, and if you have a royalty contract, you will continue to receive royalties. However, if the sales drop below the amount stated in your contract, your book will probably go out of print. When this happens, you will be able to purchase all or part of the unsold books, referred to as remainders, at the printing cost or slightly more. All rights, including the copyright, will revert to you. Sometimes a rights reversion is not an automatic procedure; the publisher may require a written request from you. If you decide not to purchase the remainders, you will no longer receive royalties and the publishing house will dispose of the books at their discretion.

Agents

If you have an agent, the agent will review your contract and make a decision on its terms and acceptance before having you sign it.

A literary agent is an author's business representative. As such, an agent's main objectives are commercial, but it is also his or her responsibility to protect the client's best interests. Agents usually do not take on new authors as clients until after they have published their first book.

If you decide to engage an agent, make sure you check out that person's track record. You will want to find out all you can about other books and clients represented by the agent, and the names of educational publishers with whom the agent has handled transactions.

A good agent will try to place your manuscript with a reliable company that publishes the kind of material you are writing—a firm with a good marketing director and one that will make you both the most money.

However, no matter how good your agent is, he or she cannot promote unsellable work, teach you how to write sellable copy, act as an editor, or sell everything you write.

Agents usually charge a commission of 12 to 15 percent and often higher for foreign negotiations. They receive the advances and royalties, deduct their commission, and then pay the balance to you.

A list of agents can be obtained through writers' organizations and from *Literary Marketplace* (LMP) at your local library. Another source is *Guide to Literary Agents & Art/Photo Reps* published by Writer's Digest Books, 1507 Dana Avenue, Cincinnati, Ohio 45207.

Quoting from Another Source

State and federal government–prepared publications, most folk literature, and material that has not been covered by copyright or on which the copyright has expired are in public domain, which means it can be used by anyone.

Under the fair-use doctrine, a limited amount of material may be quoted without permission. In order not to infringe on another author's copyright, request permission from the copyright holder. Your editor may provide you with a standard permission form and give you guidelines for its use.

Should a fee be required for the use of written material, drawings, or diagrams you wish to use, payment is usually the author's responsibility.

Credit must be given when quoting from any written source as well as from speeches and radio and television broadcasts. A credit line will insure against an accusation of plagiarism. When in doubt, check with your editor.

A reference librarian can sometimes help you find out if certain material is under copyright. A search can also be made through the Library of Congress, but this is expensive and can sometimes take months to complete.

Your contract lists your obligations and benefits. Upon receiving your copy, file it in a safe place. I have found it helpful to write pertinent information regarding my contract on the front of my file folder. Depending on the contract, I include the editor's name and company address and telephone number, due date of manuscript, number of words or pages required, disk requirements, rough artwork, and any other information that I may need during the writing process.

7

Preparing the Manuscript for Your Book

ONCE YOU RECEIVE WORD OF THE ACCEPTANCE OF your manuscript, don't wait until you get the contract to start it. Although you may have eight to twelve months to complete your material, time slips silently by and you may find yourself working under pressure to meet your deadline. It will, no doubt, take several rewrites, especially on your first book, so allow yourself extra time. The old rules about term papers you wrote in high school still apply: Allow enough time for each phase of the project.

One helpful tool might be to make up a work chart'. Your contract tells you the number of words your manuscript is to contain. After you figure out the number of words you type to a page, you can figure the number of typed pages you will need by then dividing the number of words per page into the total number of required words. You can now decide how many pages, or chapters, per day or week you will need to write to complete your project on time.

You will also want to plan extra time for editing, rewriting, and

Work Chart

Manuscript words required by contract	40,000
Number of words per page	250

40,000 ÷ 250 = 120 pages

Months before manuscript due: *8*

Allow *one month* for research and preparation

Allow *one month* for editing and preparing the manuscript package

120 pages ÷ 6 months = 20 pages per month

20 pages ÷ 4 weeks = 5 pages per week

producing the final copy. Try setting realistic daily or weekly goals for yourself and then strive to meet them.

At this point you should have already developed a detailed outline and have a good file started. This chapter contains some general, accepted standards that will guide you on the preparation of your manuscript. However, some publishers provide a handbook or manual giving exact details on manuscript preparation for their company. It is important to follow it closely.

Paper Selection

All submissions must be on 8½ × 11, white bond paper, with #20 the preferred weight. Editors do not want to see offbeat colors and sizes. Onionskin or erasable bond paper should never be used. It may be more economical to use lower grade or recycled paper for all of your early drafts.

Do not use letterhead stationery for your manuscript (you can for your cover letter, but it is not necessary).

Before You Start

I have found that when starting a first draft, it works best to set up the format as it will be for the submission copy. This will save you time reformatting and will let you see at the beginning how the final copy will look.

You may be one of those talented people who is able to compose your first draft on the word processor or typewriter, or you may find using a pencil to write up your first draft works best for you. Be sure to keep a copy of all drafts and outlines.

If you are using a word processor, be sure your printout is letter quality as dot matrix printers are not acceptable by publishers.

When using a typewriter, put in a new ribbon before starting the final copy to ensure a clear, clean manuscript. You can use correction fluid on your copy and then have professional copies made at a print shop. Most copying machines make copies that are difficult to distinguish from the original.

My first five books were written with a typewriter, but I had a problem keeping the right margin even and keeping from going beyond the bottom page margin. To eliminate this problem, I made a backing sheet by drawing a 1¼-inch margin on all four sides of a piece of white paper and a line across the center for the title line. I used a marking pen to make heavy lines, and then by placing this behind my typing paper, I had a clear guideline.

Some editors may prefer to see chapters or sections of your manuscript as they are completed. This helps them see that you are making progress on the book or projects, and, if needed, it provides a way for them to make suggestions, additions, or deletions as you go along. This process will save you valuable time in rewriting.

Writing Your Manuscript

Set up the margins so you have at least a 1¼-inch margin on all sides of your paper.

Type "Introduction" and each chapter and chapter number one-third down from the top margin in either uppercase or upper- and lowercase letters. Center chapter headings on the next line.

Your manuscript should be double spaced throughout with the standard indentation of five spaces. Print on one side of the paper only.

In the upper right-hand corner of the first page type the total word count of your manuscript. With a typewriter, you can estimate the count of elite type at 250 words with a twenty-five-line page. With pica type the word count is about 200. Count the words on one or two full pages and use this number to figure the total count. Most word processors give you an automatic word count.

Page one is the first page of your introduction. Page two, and each page thereafter (except for chapter openers), starts two double spaces down from the top margin. Start a new page for each chapter. Number the pages consecutively in the upper right-hand corner. If your word processor prints page numbers only at the bottom of the page, this is usually acceptable.

Each activity or reproducible sheet should be typed on a new page. After preparing the first two or three activity pages, you may want to send them to your editor for feedback.

If your material contains short stories, such as those for story boards, flannelgraphs, or puppets, you will want to make sure each has a beginning, a middle, and an end.

Title Page et al.

The title, copyright, dedication, and acknowledgment pages, and the preface, foreword, and table of contents are called the front matter. All books will contain a title page, a copyright page, a table of contents, and an introduction. The others may or may not be appropriate for your particular book.

The title, either in uppercase or upper- and lowercase letters, is centered halfway down the page. Below the title type your name. If there is a cowriter, type on one line the person's name that is to appear first on the book and the other person's name on the next line. Also indicate if they get equal billing. If you are using a pseudonym, mention this in your cover letter. You may also want to notify your bank and post office.

Copyright Page

The copyright page appears on the reverse side of the title page. It is prepared by the publishing house, and the copyright is registered by them in accordance with your contract. Credit lines for quoted material usually go here, or on the acknowledgment page.

Dedication Page

The dedication page is optional. It should be typed on a separate page and kept simple. If you are cowriting or the illustrator is a coauthor, both of you can make a dedication.

Acknowledgment Page

An acknowledgment page will appear if you wish to express appreciation to people or organizations who have helped you with the book in some way. This is where you give credit to, or acknowledge, your sources.

Table of Contents

The heading "Contents" is centered one-third down from the top of the page and is also double spaced. Titles and headings in the text must be worded exactly as they are on the contents page. Corresponding book page numbers will be added by the editor.

The title, copyright, dedication, and acknowledgment pages are not numbered. Number your contents pages in small roman numerals starting with the number *v* if a dedication and acknowledgment page are included in your book.

Foreword

The foreword is written by someone else (not the author of the book) who is an expert or is knowledgeable in the subject of your book. A few words of introduction written by a well-known person in the field can enhance the validity of your book.

Preface

A preface states the purpose for your book, but if this information is incorporated into your introduction, you do not need it.

Introduction to Your Book

If you included the introduction with your proposal, you may need only to expand on it. I find that it is easier to write the final introduction if I wait until I have finished the manuscript. Then I can add any areas that I might not have covered.

As mentioned in chapter 4, the introduction is your selling point for the book.

Material that follows the text of your manuscript is referred to as the end or back matter and may consist of one or more of the following: footnotes or endnotes, appendix, bibliography, glossary, and index. The type of material you are writing will determine which, if any, of these are to be included, and the guidelines will usually be provided by your editor.

Index

In most cases an index can be very helpful and often is essential. However, in books such as teacher aid books or workbooks, the contents pages are usually sufficient. Generally your editor takes care of the indexing if it is to be included. A few publishers charge against your royalties if they prepare the index, but it has been my experience that most do not.

Final Copy

After you have written and edited your last rough draft and feel it is ready for the editor, it is time to prepare the final copy of your manuscript. To make sure your manuscript will make a good impression on your editor, you will want to present it with as few errors as possible.

To save printing out additional copies, you may wish to prepare the final copy and have copies printed or photocopied (usually two are requested) to send to your editor.

Disks

You may be asked to submit both the hard copy and disk. The disk will need to be compatible with the publisher's. Each pub-

Book Format

Front matter
Title page
Copyright page
Dedication page
Acknowledgment page
Table of contents
Foreword
Preface
Introduction

Back matter
Appendix
Glossary
Bibliography
Index

lisher has its own guidelines for submitting material on disks. Although it is an additional expense for you, they may want each chapter or part on a separate disk. Guidelines for submitting computer-generated artwork will also vary with each project.

Business Cards

It is not necessary to include business cards with proposals or manuscripts. You probably will not have need for them when you first start writing.

Later, if you decide to write for publishers on a work-for-hire basis, you may want to have business cards as well as letterhead stationery and matching envelopes printed for contacting publishing houses.

Artwork

Unless you are an artist, you will probably not need to be concerned about the art. However, if you are to include rough drawings, photographs, or charts, you will be given guidelines on how to prepare and include these in your package. Artwork is discussed in chapter 5.

Do not leave a space for artwork; attach drawings, or make notations regarding artwork in your manuscript. Usually figure numbers are placed *in the margin* and an illustration sheet is included.

If you feel you have not made something clear in the text, you can describe your idea for the illustration on a separate sheet of paper.

Activity Sheets — Special Guidelines

Activity sheets have their own special requirements for publication. Here are some tips I've found helpful.

• If you are writing activity sheets or worksheets, each one usually teaches one skill per page and each stands alone. Focus on the skill to be taught (junior and senior high worksheets may cover more than one page).

• Loose activity or lab-type sheets are usually prepared for duplicating and are called blackline masters. They may be sold packaged loose or bound as books.

• Workbooks that are to be written in by students are called consumables. If the books are to be used by students as a guide with the answers written on a separate sheet of paper, the book is a nonconsumable text.

• With workbooks and worksheets, you need to leave space for the student's name. You will also want to consider the time required to complete the worksheets; however, this will depend upon the grade level for which you are preparing the material.

• Think creatively, include variety, and make the material inviting. Worksheets and workbooks should be attractive and challenging, yet appropriate for the grade level intended. The page should not appear crowded, and space for artwork needs to be considered. You will want more white space on each page when preparing materials for younger children.

• You should write directions as clearly and briefly as possible. If convenient, try to test your material with both adults and students to see if you have made clear what the student is supposed to do. It helps, too, to observe as they read and do the worksheet in order to be able to revise if necessary to clarify some areas.

• While questions are fresh in your mind, it is advisable to write your answer key immediately after finishing each activity page.

• Include variety in your puzzles, logical thinking, fill in the blank, and multiple-choice activities. Carefully proofread every piece of material, as you are the only one who knows what answer you are expecting.

Cover Letter

A cover letter is the last part of the manuscript package you write. Make it brief, including only what is necessary. However, you may also wish to extend your appreciation to your editor and express your satisfaction in working on the project.

If you haven't already, start thinking about your next book. Work on a query or outline, or start a file.

8

From Manuscript to Book

WHAT HAPPENS AFTER ALL THE TYPING IS DONE? Now that you have your final copy completed and have finished the final editing and made corrections, you are ready to prepare your manuscript package for mailing, editing, and publication.

Manuscript Package

Check through your package to make sure it is complete and all pages are in the correct order. Frequently when you have copies made at a print shop, you will discover a missing page or a blank sheet of paper, so check everything carefully.

Although all items may not apply to your package, here is a checklist to help you:

Front matter: title page, dedication, foreword, preface; introduction; manuscript pages; glossary; bibliography; appendix; rough drawings or photocopies of artwork (if you are also providing actual illustrations, be sure to include a photocopy of each, and a caption list); permission forms; disks.

This is one of the few times you do not send an SASE, but if you wish to know if your material has arrived safely, send a self-addressed, stamped (SAS) postcard. On separate lines on the back of the postcard, type the title of your manuscript, received by, and date received (see sample).

You will, of course, want to make sure you meet your deadline by allowing time for the material to reach your editor. Planning so it will arrive several days before the contracted deadline always makes a good impression.

Pack and Mail

Do not fold, punch, staple, paper clip, or place your manuscript in a binder or folder. Never put manuscripts in a loose-leaf ring binder. Send it in a flat box such as a typing paper box or a large padded envelope. If mailed in a padded envelope, a loose rubber band can be placed around the manuscript.

If disks are included in your package, each one should contain your name, the title, and chapter heading and number. If there is more than one disk, label the disks one of four, two of four, and so on. Your editor, or the publisher's manual for authors, or the contract itself will give you specifics for creating and sending disks if they are to be included. Disks should be placed in cardboard or plastic disk holders or wrapped well in cardboard and placed on top of the hard copy submission. Tape the box securely. Packages wrapped in paper and tied with string or secured with household cellophane tape may not be acceptable by all postal services.

Type an adhesive-backed label addressed to your editor and another label with your return address. Attach the labels in the appropriate location on either the box or the envelope.

You can send your manuscript package by first-class mail, first-

Self-Addressed, Stamped (SAS) Postcard
(message side)

Title: RECYCLING ACTIVITIES FOR THE PRIMARY GRADES
Received by:
Date:

class Priority Mail (arrives in two days—*usually*), or United Postal Service. Overnight or two-day UPS can be used if you are pressed for time; however, it is considerably more expensive. Three-day service is cheaper, and the package can be tracked. Registering the package is not necessary since you have retained a copy, and you will be assured of the date of your project's arrival when you receive your SAS postcard. Your editor or editorial assistant may also send you a letter informing you of your manuscript's arrival and stating that your editor will get back to you as soon as possible after reading it.

Revising and Editing

Your publisher bears the responsibility for designing the cover, choosing a final title, designing interior pages, and making other manufacturing and marketing decisions, but don't assume that your job is finished once you send in your manuscript package. It is a rare occasion when a manuscript requires no revisions, additions, or corrections by the author. No matter how many times we read over our manuscripts and how carefully we check, it is easy to overlook some errors. A paragraph or description may seem clear to you, the author, but to your editor, portions of it or even entire paragraphs may need to be rewritten for clarification.

The editing process varies with each publishing house. In some cases, you may receive a copy of your manuscript containing the copy editor's marks and notes, either written in the text or margin, or both.

To better understand the copy editor's changes you will want to familiarize yourself with standard proofreader's marks. An explanation of proofreader's marks can be found in dictionaries, encyclopedias, and in some books on writing for publication.

Occasionally, there will be "flags" (small pieces of paper attached to and extending beyond the right-hand side of the page), with editorial notes added. If you feel changes need to be made, such as adding or deleting a paragraph or activity, this is the time to indicate such changes.

Before the printing of your book, the galleys, or proofs, may also be sent to you to check, but mostly for typographical errors. Small corrections can still be made at this point, but you should not make any major changes or you may be required to pay for the cost of doing so. Corrections on proofs are always put in the margin, left or right, next to the line of type in which the correction is to be made.

In some cases, you may receive copies of the illustrations to check, not for the style of illustration, but for accuracy.

It is important that you return copies of text and art as soon as possible, because editors, artists, and the production crew all work under tight deadlines.

Follow-up phone calls from editorial staff are common, as they save time and postage. The illustrator may also contact you to clarify your rough drawings or a description in the text that is to be illustrated.

As an author, you must be willing to revise as many times as the editor feels is necessary. Revising is not an exciting part of the writing process, and you would probably prefer to spend the time working on your next project, but it is necessary. Educational editors are very knowledgeable about the field. They meet with and listen to teachers, attend conferences, study the market, make themselves aware of the competition, and are familiar with educational trends; therefore, they are determined to make your book one that teachers will buy and use.

In some of my books, I neither saw the galleys nor was I involved in the editing process. It was the policy of the publishing house to send manuscripts to an outside, free-lance editor who was an expert in that particular field. The outside editor did the editing and made the necessary revisions. On the other hand, with other companies, I often was involved in both the editing and the rewriting, had input for some illustrations, and had the opportunity to check and even to make small changes in some of the art.

When only a few pages of your manuscript require revisions and time is pressing, your editor may ask you to fax the corrected pages.

Sometime during this period of copyediting, revision, typesetting, and printing, you may also be asked to write copy and to send a photograph of yourself for the jacket flap or back cover. If this is your first experience in writing about yourself, reading the copy on several different books will help you. Publishers may wish to send a news release on your book (and maybe a photo of the book and/or one of you) to newspaper publishers, journals and magazines, and radio/TV stations in your general area that give attention to books in education. If so, you will be asked to provide a list of media and their addresses. Be sure to provide names of important educational media, not just the usual TV talk shows. It is also important that you respond to these requests as soon as possible.

Future Assignments

If you have ideas for other projects, submit them to your editor now — don't wait until your book comes out. Once you have established a harmonious working relationship with an editor, even if you have an option clause in your contract, you may be invited to submit other ideas.

If your editor is pleased with your work, he or she may suggest a follow-up book or the possibility of developing your book into a series, or you may be invited to submit an outline to fill a special need for the publisher's list. Once they have published your first book, editors are usually anxious to have you continue to submit ideas and become one of their producing authors — to your advantage, too.

Marketing

Editors are special people; they *do* care about you as well as your book and they want your book to be the best it can possibly be. Some editors also handle the marketing; other companies have marketing directors. Among the many things I have had editors/marketing directors do for me is to presell my book, sell it to a book club, negotiate for sale of the foreign language rights, convert measurement to the metric system and sell to the Canadian or European markets, approach me with suggestions for writing another book, set up displays at conferences and conventions and spend several days in the booth pushing and selling my book (as well as their other new books), and set up a special table in the booth for me to autograph my book. Your publisher may be in a position to do all or none of these or a few, based on your ideas and cooperation.

Author's Copies

The average time for producing a book after the manuscript is received by the publisher is about one year, but sometimes less. Your editor may give you a tentative publishing date or it may be written into your contract.

Soon after your book is published, you will receive your author's copies. Your contract usually states the number—five to twelve copies on average. Usually, you will be able to purchase extra copies for your own use or to give away, but not to sell, at a 40 percent discount. Only a few publishers will make arrangements for you to purchase books for resale (see chapter 18 on promoting your book). Depending on the publishing company and the marketing plan, your book may be simultaneously published in both hardcover and paperback.

Your Beautiful New Book

It is impossible to explain the joy that floods over you when you open that long-awaited package from your publisher and hold in your hands your very first book—your book! But as you continue to marvel at its existence and carefully turn one page after the other, you realize that many very creative, caring people pooled their talents and worked many long hours to produce your book, which in reality, is their book, too. I have never been able to visualize how my completed book would look, even after seeing a rough sketch of the cover in some cases. My first book was beautiful to behold and far beyond anything I had ever imagined or expected, and the same can be said for each of my succeeding books. I have never been disappointed in the appearance of the cover, interior design, or the artwork.

Your editor is anxious to hear your reaction to your book, so call or send a handwritten note immediately.

When your publishing company publishes its catalog, annually or semiannually, ask to be sent a copy. If your book did not make the catalog deadline, a catalog insert may list your book along with the company's other new books. Seeing your book listed or shown in a publisher's catalog is another thrill that comes to a first-time published author. Equally exciting are published reviews of your book. Your publisher may send you clippings or you may discover them yourself in favorite journals.

Fan Mail

I never expected to receive fan mail regarding my educational books or other materials. For some reason, I felt that only children and young people wrote to authors who had published picture books or YA novels. However, I have received several letters sent to me via my publishers from teachers, parents, and, yes, children. Their letters contained welcome words of praise. One child wrote commenting on one of my activity books and another on a nonfiction science book—she even asked some questions to which I eagerly replied.

Comments from fellow teachers are perhaps the most gratifying to receive. Just knowing that busy teachers take the time to write, to know they are sharing my ideas with young people, and that I, as an author, have in some small way contributed to the education of children, is extremely rewarding.

9

Adjunct Learning Materials: Selling and Submitting Nonbook Ideas

THE MAJORITY OF NONBOOK MATERIALS FOR THE EDucational market seem to be either produced in-house or assigned by the publisher to their regular free-lance authors and illustrators to develop. However, since publishing companies are always looking for fresh ideas, there will continue to be a place for good teacher-developed and classroom-tested material. Many publishers of supplemental material welcome free-lance submissions that evolve out of a need within the classroom and that have been *tested* and revised by the teacher-developer. In demand are products that

• Are self-help, self-checking—materials students can do on their own and that have answer keys so they can check their own work, or games or puzzles that won't work unless the student gives the right answer to the clues or questions.

• Allow for individualized learning—graduated levels of materials that progress from easy to more difficult so each student can work at his or her individual ability.

• Feature a cross-curriculum approach—materials that provide a continuity across the curriculum; integrating a topic or study unit into many areas of the curriculum, such as math, reading, spelling, history.

• Are literature based—materials that in some way introduce or reinforce language and literature, such as fairy tales, drama, and poetry.

• Introduce or reinforce basic skills—supplemental material relating to shapes, colors, and counting or addition, subtraction, and vowels.

• Provide for special needs students—interesting and exciting materials for slow learners, students with learning problems, or non–English-speaking students.

• Include multicultural diversity—learning about foods, language, celebrations, and holidays of *many* other cultures.

• Offer enrichment for gifted students—exciting and challenging materials for students who are ready to go beyond the average grade-level material.

• Offer something different—a *new* way of presenting curriculum units or any body of knowledge, an improvement of some kind, or what seems to be a new and innovative idea.

Class testing is essential. It is important to test and retest your product, especially games, before you send it to a company for consideration.

You will also want to take into consideration your product's need for a teacher's guide, instructions for its use, game rules, suggestions for ways it can extend certain learning experiences, or how it can be used in other areas of the curriculum.

As you think about your product, try to answer the following questions before you approach a product developer. These five questions will also help you in writing up the purpose or objectives of your idea.

1. What learning experiences will it teach or reinforce?
2. What exactly will it do that no other product does?
3. How will the user benefit from my product?
4. For whom is the material geared to help teach, train, or educate?
5. Why or how will it appeal to this age or grade level?

Manipulative Materials

Manipulative learning aids have proven to be successful since first manufactured in the United States by Milton Bradley Company. They were originally developed for use in kindergarten, but educators soon discovered they could be used effectively with students in other grades as well. This is a broad area, but puzzles, table games, board games, and cards are among the most common.

Games, puzzles, and card activities must be appropriate for the age level audience and should be challenging—but not frustrating—to the user. And, of course, educational toys and games should teach as well as entertain.

Since some board games may require skills in logical thinking, reading, counting, or the use of play money, it is more difficult to create this type of game for young children who have *not* acquired these skills. Pictures, colors, and arrows can be used in place of written directions for games aimed at younger, nonreading students.

Manufacturing companies only buy and produce what they feel the market wants and needs, that is, what will sell! You, as an instructional materials developer, must present to the company what you know teachers want, although the producer may not yet know it, and convince them of its financial potential.

Jigsaw puzzles—either wooden or heavy cardboard—must have some unique feature or purpose.

Cards—playing, task, flash, matching, and sequence cards—are found in most classrooms. Picture cards, cut into three or four pieces, may be used to reinforce a study unit. They come in sets, are usually based on a theme, and are aimed at preschool to third grade. They are self-correcting (only the right piece fits), but developing such a set is time-consuming and not as easy as one would think.

Table games and activities can be for individual or class use. A game might relate to math, geography, or any area of study. A type of bingo game might reinforce the teaching of a concept such as colors, shapes, or opposites.

Protecting Your Product

It should be noted that product developers and publishers are not always willing to work with someone whose material has already been registered with the Copyright or Patent offices. However, you can receive information on copyrights, patents, and trademarks by writing to the Copyright Office, Library of Congress, Washington, DC 20559.

As a designer of instructional aids such as nonmechanical, electronic, video, or computer learning aids, you can protect your idea with just a copyright if you want to. The following can all be copyrighted:

- Artist-created work such as drawings, illustrations, and posters
- Published reproduction of photographs and slides
- Films, television tapes, and other audiovisual productions
- Musical compositions
- Scripts and dramatic productions

Copyright—To register copyrighted material, write the Copyright Office for an application. They will require two copies of the work, along with a fee of $20, to register the copyright.

Disclosure Document—Under the disclosure program, the United States Patent Office "accepts and preserves," for a period of two years, papers referred to as "disclosure documents." These papers may be used as evidence of the date of conception of inventions. The document should contain a clear and complete explanation for making and using the invention including drawings or sketches if needed. It is then signed by the inventor and sent to the Patent Office along with a filing fee of $20. Disclosure documents are sent by many companies who manufacture products or produce audiovisual materials when one inquires about the procedure of presenting an idea.

Patents—Applying for a patent is a long and expensive process that requires the advice and expertise of a patent attorney. Patent attorneys are listed in the Yellow Pages, or Inventor's Workshop International with branches in most large cities (also found in the

Yellow Pages) has a list of recommended patent attorneys. You can visit their local "open meetings," and ask questions, purchase helpful books, and make contacts (attorneys, consultants, and fellow inventors) without joining the organization.

Trademarks—A trademark may consist of a word, phrase, person's name, picture, symbol, or any combinations of these. It is used to distinguish the products of one company from those of another. You can consult the *Trademark Register* found in most of the larger libraries to find out if there is a trademark similar to one you have in mind. Although the book lists all the registered trademarks by name in alphabetical order, you will still need to do a search through the Patent Office. Again this requires a great deal of time and expense.

Licensed Characters

Toys, articles of clothing, souvenirs, and many other items that develop out of the popularity of characters in books are usually commissioned through the publishing house.

If you feel your idea would support a licensed toy or other product, it is best to develop the character in print *first* and then it will be under copyright. It is difficult to create and develop a successful character without it first becoming popularized, thus providing a ready-made marketing outlet.

Yet, it is not impossible. You may find a publisher who sees the potential and will publish a book along with a character, but these are usually picture or novelty book publishers.

Contacting a Manufacturer

If you have a product idea and wish to sell it to a company, first do your homework. Start by sending for catalogs, visiting stores that produce products similar to yours, and studying the competition. You don't want to duplicate material already on the market unless yours has unique features—improves the learning scope, is more compact, or can be used by a different age group.

The procedure for sending inquiries and materials to a company that produces nonbook materials is *much different* from sending material to an educational book publisher. You do not want to give away your idea. Unfortunately, this is an area where, since it is hard to prove who had the ideas first, one must be cautious in divulging too much information. Do not send models or drawings until you have something concrete from a producer such as a signed disclosure document or a written agreement of some type.

Some companies buy the idea itself and pay a flat fee. They may or may not develop it. Other companies may pay by giving gift certificates for their catalog products in exchange for your idea. Some companies have contests where teachers send in their ideas, and the winners receive a certain amount of catalog items of their choice—Lakeshore Learning Materials is one of these. Information and rules are found *only* in their catalog.

Teachers who have submitted product proposals say that in order to protect your product idea, it is best to first send a brief letter of inquiry, mentioning only the broad category of what you have to offer, such as a set of science-related jigsaw puzzles or a game for teaching the names of states and their capitals. Ask for the company's guidelines for submitting ideas for new products, and query whether the firm would be interested in more details and a photograph or drawing of your teacher-developed idea. When mailing your letter of inquiry, register the letter and ask for a signed return receipt.

Even sending an SASE will not guarantee you a reply to your inquiry, because some companies will not respond. After a reasonable waiting time, send your idea to another product developer. Belief in your product and perseverance are essential if you expect to see results in this field.

If you receive a positive response to your letter, send only what is required. The company may ask to see your finished product; a drawing with detailed instructions for constructing your product plus a guide for its use; or a photograph and description of your project. Protect yourself and your product by making sure your name, address, and the date appear on every written page, drawing, photograph, and on the product itself.

Some companies may only give a response if you send the completed product. If you live near the company, you may want to call for an appointment to show your product. However, you should do this only after you have sent the letter of inquiry so you will have a record of the date and the letters you sent and received.

If the completed product is to be sent, prepare it neatly and attractively. You should never send your original, nor should you send the game your students have been using in the classroom. Since the product developer will want to test play the game (or other product) make sure all the required pieces, such as dice, game pieces, spinners, and tokens are included—plus rules and/or directions for its use. Place small pieces in small, plastic zip-type bags.

Along with a clearly written description of your product, send a list of all the parts needed. This will help give the producer an idea of the manufacturer's cost. Depending on your product, you may also need to include drawings, slides or photographs, and any directions or rules that are needed.

Packaging Your Product

Packaging can be an important sales tool. Manufacturers spend millions of dollars trying to come up with the best way to package their products. If you have developed a game, puzzle, or learning kit, you will need to prepare the entire project and make it look as attractive as possible. Then place it in a box with the name (such as Pathways to State Capitals) neatly printed on the box top. If you have had professional training as an artist, you may want to add a simple illustration.

You can purchase plain white boxes at gift and party stores. One with a gold or red lid might be appropriate.

Experiment by placing a piece of felt or crushed velvet or satin in the bottom of a box that is a little larger than your item. Select colors and textures that will complement your product best.

Mailing Your Product

Depending on the weight, send your sample product first class, Priority Mail, or by United Parcel Service. Place your letter inside the box along with a copy of the original letter you sent and the one you received from the company. It is wise to insure the parcel and ask for a return receipt. Be sure to enclose enough postage to ensure the return of your material. This may be expensive, but it will help protect you and your product.

Student Activity Sheets

Activity sheets, also called worksheets, if not in book form, are packaged loose in a package of twenty or more and focus on a particular skill, developmental task, or area of the curriculum. They are designed to be reproduced. Activity sheets are less structured than a workbook, and you can be more creative in designing them. Each sheet contains minimal directions, and the younger the child the more art that appears on the page. Be sure to leave space for the student's name, and if you cannot do the artwork, leave a space to indicate where art should go. You can draw stick figures or describe the art in a bubble.

If you feel there is an area that has not been addressed in the material that is available, or have ideas on how to improve or present worksheets in a different way, query the publisher and send a few samples.

If you have an innovative way of packaging this item, mention it to your producer or publisher.

Blackline masters can be produced on a computer. See chapter 5 on computer graphics.

Illustrated Material

Charts, maps, posters, study prints, bulletin board borders, or printed cut-out or punch-out decorating materials are areas a teacher/illustrator may want to investigate. If you are not artistic, you might want to brainstorm some ideas with your school art teacher.

Motivational material such as stickers, stamps, certificates, and rewards also benefit from the talents of a creative artist.

You may want to query Rand McNally (maps and atlases) and B. Shackman & Company (a major producer of stickers).

Query first and ask if you can send drawing or samples. They may only want to see pencil or pen and ink sketches for initial evaluation. When you send art, remember to send *copies only* (see chapter 5).

Audiovisuals

Technology has given us many new audiovisual formats for learning and reinforcing concepts, basic skills, and other studies. Audiovisual media are as common as books in today's classrooms. With advances in microcomputers and video, and computerized teaching, a vast array of opportunities have opened up for teacher-authors and teacher-illustrators.

Educational audiovisual materials include filmstrips, videos, overhead transparencies, audiotapes, and cassettes. Cassette/book sets usually come out after the book is published. If you are commissioned to do audiotapes or cassettes, you can ask the producer for a sample product. The sample along with the company's guidelines will help you in preparing your material.

First send a query and an SASE for guidelines. A producer may want to see an outline, sample script, a story board, or all three.

For a complete list of audiovisual markets, check R. R. Bowker's annual edition of *Audio Video Market Place,* which can be found in the reference section of most college and larger local libraries.

Film and Television Scripts

Television and film scripts are generally sold through agents. Yet some material occasionally comes in through the back door, for example, via a person who is well known professionally. If you have a best-selling book, have won several awards, and have had good reviews, your publisher may be able to auction the film or television rights to your book. But unless you know someone in the field, your chances of breaking into this market depend on your network of professional contacts.

Although written for professional filmmakers, a helpul guide on films is Renée Harmon's *The Beginning Filmmaker's Business Guide,* published by Walker and Company. It contains information on finding a distributor, writing proposals, negotiating contracts, and the major studios.

The film and television industry is a very complex business. This, along with the fact that it is almost impossible to prove who had an idea first, especially if the script is based on events that have made nationwide news, behooves anyone trying to sell their script to take extra precautions. Professional ethics do not always appear to be a strong point among those in the entertainment industry.

The Writer's Guild allows you to write only one thing for television without joining their organization. Write to the guild for information (see the appendix).

Multimedia Kits

Multimedia or learning kits are made up of materials that focus on one concept or study and contain a variety of related materials. The audience is primarily preschool through third grade students, but many are also utilized in high school and college courses, too, especially in the sciences. A concept kit on geometric shapes might contain a Big Book or picture book, filmstrip, puppets, games, and activity sheets. Maps, an atlas, charts, study prints, supplies for making a relief map, and a video, audio, or disk plus software are materials one could find in a geography kit. Assorted rocks, samples of soil, and illustrated charts on rock formations might be in a kit for a learning unit in geology. Kit materials are packaged in an attractive "place for everything" container that is easy to carry and store.

If you have an idea for a learning kit, query the company with your idea. Several people may contribute to a kit. You may wish to submit the idea and write the teacher's guide, illustrate activity sheets, or write the text for a filmstrip.

Among the companies that offer a variety of learning kits in their catalogs are: Lakeshore Learning Materials, Nasco, Edmund Scientific, and Carolina Biological Supply.

Filmstrips are the primary product of the Society for Visual Education (SVE); CLEARVUE/eav looks for filmstrips, slide sets, and videotapes; and Gateway Productions, Inc. produces educational audiovisual materials (see the market directory in the appendix).

Plays

Breaking in is the hard part when writing for the theater, because it is almost impossible to publish your play until it has been performed.

The normal procedure in sending scripts for plays is to send an outline along with your query. The next step is to prepare and send a first draft. After editing and revising, the final draft is prepared. Some editors are very specific as to the number of pages, lines to a page, and words per line.

You will want to think about the stage directions as well as the dialogue and narration. Plays for children should be simple to produce and require only a few props, costumes, and special effects. Mime is frequently used—you don't need a real fire hose with water, mime it! The biggest demand is for one-act plays.

You might want to consider writing a book of short plays that you have used successfully in your classroom. Check out several books on children's plays from the library and study the format.

Other possibilities for anyone interested in plays and theater might be to submit patterns or designs for simple costumes or create a set of generic props for use in the classroom or touring theater groups.

Two good resources for anyone interested in writing for this market are *PLAYS, The Drama Magazine for Young People,* 120 Boylston Street, Boston, MA 02116 and Children's Story Scripts, Baymax Productions, 2219 W. Olive Avenue, Suite 130, Burbank, CA 91506. Both have excellent guidelines.

Payment for Nonbook Material

If your idea is accepted you may have to agree to sell all rights to your product. There is a wide variation in payment depending on the company, the type of product, and the age level.

Some companies do pay royalties, and advances usually come after you have worked on a few projects for a company. However, the majority of companies pay flat fees, which vary greatly due to the diversity of the materials and the sellability of the product. The range may be from several hundred to several thousand dollars.

Classroom tools, games, and puzzles bring a flat fee of $500 to $5,000.

Activity sheet producers are usually paid a flat fee of $25 to $100 per page or by the set.

Audiovisual pay rates will, for the most part, be based on royalties. For writers and songwriters and for recording musicians, the standard royalty is 50 percent net.

For audiocassettes the scale would be a flat fee of $2,000 to $20,000 for sets, royalties 5 to 15 percent, advances from $1,000 to $2,000.

Film and television payment scales vary. There are so many variables in this field that payment is most often negotiated on an individual basis.

Multimedia kits usually bring a flat fee of $1,000 to $5,000 depending on your contribution to the kit. With a few companies, royalties might be considered.

Due to the large number of times a children's play is performed, theaters often pay a flat fee rather than royalties and then return all rights to the author at the close of a run. Payment is from a few hundred to a few thousand dollars, depending on the size of the theater.

In other cases, a royalty is paid each time the play is performed.

Competition in the educational, nonbook product business is keen, but if you have a well-developed and unique idea that meets a specific educational need, and you present it in a professional manner, there is a good possibility of seeing your product sold, produced, and used in classrooms around the world.

10

Writing and Selling Curriculum-related Books and Textbooks

CURRICULUM-RELATED BOOKS SUPPLEMENT THE IN-formation in textbooks used in the classroom. Usually they are nonfiction, but with younger children they may occasionally be fiction. They are written to enrich or extend the topic of study, which is limited within the textbook. All areas of the basic curriculum are included in this category as well as books on health-related topics including AIDS, drugs, smoking, alcohol, exercise, and nutrition; environmental issues; ethnic studies; and career choices.

Curriculum-oriented publishers usually only sell to schools and libraries while other trade publishers will have a crossover market, which means they also sell to bookstores and other juvenile book outlets. Both series and single titles and hardcover and paperback are published for this genre.

If curriculum-related books are your special interest, check your school and library shelves and your school's textbook library to find out if there is a need for the type of book you want to write. At our county school textbook library for social studies is a nonfiction book on the California missions to supplement the unit in the textbook on California history; there is another book on the La Brea tar pits (located in the center of Los Angeles) explaining how the fossils, dug from the deep pits located on museum grounds, are cleaned and identified. I discovered this book, by a Los Angeles author, in the science unit. Local school textbook libraries often add their own reading choices. I made an appointment with the media supervisor, and after presenting a short "book talk" on my book, *Story Sparklers,* and how it could supplement and enhance the reading program, donated a copy to the media/textbook library.

You should also check *Books in Print,* publishers' catalogs, teacher supply stores, and a good college library to see how many books there are on your chosen subject before you query a publisher or start your manuscript. You will want to make a note of the grade levels, publishers, authors, and copyright dates for any books you find on your subject or topic. Again, you should write for publishers' guidelines and catalogs and send only the materials required, such as an outline and sample chapters.

To mention just one area of the curriculum, no one denies the need for increased geography education. Results from the first national Assessment of Educational Progress (1990) showed twelfth graders responded correctly to only 57 percent of multiple-choice geography questions. To compound this situation, world geography is changing rapidly today. Finding a way to meet this challenge may be just the area for you! The same can be said for math, science, and reading.

You will find that reading association magazines, published for every area of the curriculum—among them *Science Teacher* from the National Science Teachers Association and *Language Arts* from the National Council of Teachers of English—are helpful sources filled with articles that can spark writing and publishing ideas (see the listing in the appendix).

Research

Writing curriculum-related books requires a great deal of research and it is time-consuming, yet it makes for a good book and you can save the unused research material and recycle it into other educational areas (see chapter 12, "Recycling Your Ideas and Your Research"). It is important that you record the source of all your research information. If a name, place, or quote is questionable, your editor will ask you to substantiate the information. With certain types of books, publishers may also require a bibliography. You will want to record the necessary information along with any special illustrations, models, maps, graphs, or photographs you discover during your research.

If you live near a college or university, take advantage of their library services for research. You may find *A Guide to the College Library* by Christopher Lee Philips (Walker and Company) helpful when doing research. He recommends the *Sears List of Subject Headings,* the *Library of Congress Subject Headings,* and two indexes: the *Educational Index* and *Resources in Higher Education,* for people interested in writing for preschool through seventh grade.

When I do library research, I not only make a note of the source but also include the call number and the initials of the library (since I use three libraries and each is located in a different city). On newspaper and magazine clippings, I note the date and the name of the newspaper or publication.

In a magazine article I did on beetles, I had mentioned the strength of the Hercules beetle, stating it could crush a soft drink can between its two powerful horns. My editor said he did not doubt the possibility, but asked if I had any proof for the statement. Although I had never observed this creature's magnificent test of strength, I had cut from a newspaper a picture showing the beetle in action and I had noted the source and publication date. I made a photocopy and sent it to my editor.

After studying several publishers' catalogs and guidelines, you will have a better understanding of the editor's needs when you are ready to prepare your proposal. If an editor asks to see the completed manuscript, such as a biography that you are proposing to fit into their series, you will want to read as many of the books in the series as possible. If you cannot find copies in your school or the public library, write and ask the publisher for a sample copy. By reading and carefully checking the copies, you will then have a good overview of what is expected. Note the number of pages, chapter format, and number of illustrations, drawings, or photographs.

Many publishers want true-to-life books about different cultures or ethnic groups. However, most publishers prefer that authors be part of the culture about which they are writing, but some will accept "as told to" books. An example would be writing about a specific Native American tribe from the point of view of a person within the tribe. You, as the author, would record interviews and background data, maintaining the facts, flavor, and customs, and then supplement it with your own research.

Just Us Books publishes books only on African-American themes—*Great Women, A Book of Black Heroes, First Book About Africa,* and *Afro-Bets ABC Book;* Childrens Press's cultural folktales are packaged singly or with a cassette; Dillon Press has a series called *Discovering Our Heritage* on many different countries (you may be able to add to this series; query and ask for a catalog); and Scholastic publishes multicultural books as well as favorite picture books in Spanish—*The Carrot Seed, Corduroy,* and *Giant Dinosaurs.*

MultiCultural Review, Horn Book, and *Publisher's Weekly* are good sources for book reviews. If you cannot find copies in your college or public library, ask the children's librarian if you can browse through his or her desk copy. Our local children's librarian feels that "kids of all cultures need to see themselves in literature. Literature needs to be multiracial. This includes illustrations as well, and many old favorites are being revised to include all cultures in illustrations and book covers."

Nonfiction

Nonfiction books, also called "fact books," are becoming an important part of the classroom bookshelf inventory. Any topic or subject that relates information on areas of study in the classroom are possibilities. Using previously published topics or material and rewriting it at a different grade level, creating a new organization of existing information, updating books that are out of print or out of date, and providing current facts and information are open areas for nonfiction authors. Your text can be presented as straight information—just the facts, in novel form, or question and answer format.

A children's bookstore owner told me: "We need more nonfiction books for very young children. The media have made today's children more aware; they are curious about everything—they want to find out."

Biographies

Celebrity biographies are in great demand. Some publishers have biography series relating to history, inventors, scientists, or musicians, as well as contemporary figures. Finding a publisher who does biographies for the age level and in the category where your subject fits is your starting point.

Librarians and publishers today want biographies that relate true facts and do not contain fabricated dialogue. A children's librarian told me: "Youngsters want biographies that are appealing, such as *Mrs. Field's Cookies,* a recently published biography that is very popular. Also we are starting to see short chapter collections such as *Women in Baseball.*" I was also told that more biographies for younger children—kindergarten through third grade—are in demand by teachers and librarians.

True biographies require accuracy, in both characters and events. History provides the facts, which cannot be changed; therefore, you must write your book around them.

If you are writing about a baseball figure (even if you know the game well), read, interview, obtain quotes, and become knowledgeable on what takes place between players and managers, problems on the road, humorous events, and what goes on in the locker room. If writing a biography on Mozart, you will not only want to read about his birthplace, childhood, and adult life, but also about historical events of the period, and look for quotes by the composer as well as those of family members and friends.

It helps to outline in chronological order—birth and family, childhood, schooling, young adulthood, and so on—and then decide where you want to begin. This will also give you a good overview of what you plan to include in your outline to the publisher.

Chapters for biographies and nonfiction books in general will be shorter for the younger audience, sometimes only one to three pages. Regardless of grade level, each chapter needs to end with a hook (an element of suspense that makes the reader unable to put the book down until he or she finds out what happens next).

Authorized biographies are based on interviews with the person about whom you are writing. Also you will want to check books, magazines, newspapers, and other written sources. Newspaper articles, unless syndicated, are considered public domain and may be quoted from without seeking permission. For longer newspaper and magazine articles, you can paraphrase portions of the article using your own creative expression of language.

Contacting close friends, teachers, or other family members is a good method to obtain little-known and humorous information that will add a "real person" touch to your biography.

Unauthorized biographies are written with or without the co-operation of the subject. Your information then must come from published sources (usually newspapers and magazines) and through interviews with people who know or knew the figure and are willing to give you inside information.

Your publisher will furnish you with guidelines and usually a sample book in their biography series.

Photo-Essay Books

Photo or photo-essay books are illustrated with photographs. As the author, you may be able to take your own professional photographs or may wish to provide them. Query the editor with your idea, outline, and sample chapters if appropriate. Do not send photographs or slides with your manuscript. See chapter 5 for information on submitting photographs and sources for photographs.

Almost any nonfiction topic can be illustrated with photographs. Photo books on other countries, children, holidays, celebrations, government, and places of interest make facts and descriptions more realistic and accessible. Books on science topics—weather, insects, birds, and other wildlife—and social studies, careers, and geography are good subjects. Drawings, however, are preferable in some instances. Your editor will advise you.

Among the publishers of nonfiction photo-essay books are: Morrow, Lodestar, and Dillon Press.

Nonfiction Picture Books

For picture books, you should always send the complete manuscript unless the publisher's guidelines state otherwise. These books are short and easy to read and are usually thirty-two pages in length, though in some cases, they may be forty-eight pages. Do not send artwork unless you are a professional artist, and then send only what the publisher requests. This is usually a dummy with three or four pen-and-ink drawings and a copy of a finished piece of art. You can check the library for books on writing and illustrating children's books to find out how to make a dummy.

If your picture book manuscript is accepted, the publisher will usually provide the illustrator. You can, however, suggest the use of photographs if you feel this is best for your book.

Educational publishers who publish curriculum-related books may also publish picture books that supplement the subject area. You can obtain a list of juvenile publishers by sending an SASE with a first-class stamp to the Children's Book Council, 568 Broadway, Suite 404, New York, NY 10012. Check their list for names and addresses of publishers accepting manuscripts for nonfiction picture books.

Big Books

Big Books are a popular market today but not every educational publisher produces them. These picture book sets are for preschool through second or third grade. They may contain stories, rhymes, fairy tales, or information on various subjects such as the cycle of the butterfly, animals, or gardening.

The book to be used by the teacher is oversize, an average book being 14 × 19 inches and containing thirty-two pages. With a thirty-two-page book, your manuscript may be only two to three pages long. There are also early reader–type Big Books in which the page count runs higher.

The Big Book set includes smaller, individual books (one for each student). They contain the same text for the students to read and may also involve them in coloring or drawing activities.

In most cases, Big Books are first published as a picture book; however, with some publishers, the two may be published and marketed together.

If you want to write a Big Book, study the layout of those available to you. The editor's guidelines will define the requirements. Usually you will be asked to send the manuscript and a dummy. Even if you are not an artist, you may need to lay out the book with both the text and the ideas for the illustrations.

The following are among the companies that publish Big Books: Modern Curriculum Press, Bank Street, and The Wright Group. Addison-Wesley publishes Big Books for kindergarten on mathematics and literature.

Computer Books

More and more computers can be seen in classrooms today, even at the kindergarten and preschool level. Computer manuals for existing programs are produced by the developer. However, many teachers are not pleased with what is available and write their own variations on the programs.

If you want to sell your innovative, yet useful, ideas as computer books or guides, find out all you can about the programs and software being used in schools. Subscribe to journals and teacher magazines that cover computer education—*Instructor* magazine, *Technology & Learning,* and *Teaching K-8* (see chapter 14 on educational magazines).

Attending computer education fairs where you will find handouts that often contain questionnaires from companies looking for authors, speaking with the company representative, and browsing their materials and displays will give you a good insight into this writing field.

Query companies that interest you and ask for guidelines for submitting free-lance material or applying for assignments.

Textbooks

The textbook publishing industry is not an easy field to break into and it is certainly not an open market to unproven free-lance writers. Writing for this field may sometimes require a Ph.D., consultant status, and a recognized standing in a particular curriculum area. Credentials will vary depending on the grade level for which you want to write.

Knowing and understanding children and their developmental stages, school curricula, state education codes, and textbook framework, as well as how to write for a particular reading level are all necessary attributes for textbook authors.

State education codes tell you what is legal and what is illegal to include in textbooks—every superintendent in each school district of your state has a copy. State textbook framework—one for each area of the curriculum such as science and social studies—gives a suggested outline for what should be included at each grade level for that subject, and copies should be available at every school.

You may also want to consider volunteering to serve on your state textbook evaluation or adoption committee in order to increase your knowledge and qualifications for writing in this field.

Since every school in the country uses textbooks and publishers are competing for selection, textbook publishing is a big business. As most states reevaluate their school textbooks every four to six years for every subject from first grade, even kindergarten in some states, through high school, publishers must revise and update their products on a regular basis.

The author of a textbook most likely did not write *all* of the information in the book. You may want to consider becoming a contributor to a textbook. Query several textbook publishers listing your qualifications and the curriculum area for which you wish to write. A prospectus for describing your specialization is then sent to authors. Upon evaluation, you may be contracted, usually on a work for hire basis, to contribute to a textbook.

Depending on what is involved, it may take up to a year to write one chapter. Research is critical.

Today all textbooks are written at specific reading levels, which sadly is *below* grade level, and publishers issue rigid guidelines and outlines that authors are expected to follow.

Other possibilities for contributing to textbooks are writing several pages of enrichment materials, activity pages, study guides, test items, and stories for an anthology.

Payment for Curriculum-related Books

Payment and advances vary depending on the grade level, number of pages, research required, and number and type of illustrations or photographs (black-and-white or color). Experience often dictates the amount of an advance. Standard royalties are 10 percent on a hardcover book and 6 to 10 percent on paperback. Percentage is usually figured on the net price, not the list (retail). The following rates are, on the average, what one can expect.

Nonfiction
  Flat fee—$500 to $2,000
  Advance—$2,000 to $5,000
  Royalty—8 to 10 percent

Biographies
  Flat fee—$500 to $2,000
  Advance—$2,000 to $5,000
  Royalty—8 to 10 percent
  Top celebrity biographies can bring advances up to $10,000.

Photo-Essay
  Flat fee—$500 to $2,000
  Advance—$1,000 to $5,000
  Royalty—usually 8 to 10 percent if the author or the publishing house provides the photographs. Otherwise, 5 percent to author and 5 percent to the photographer.

Nonfiction Picture Books
  Flat fee—$500 to $1,000
  Advance—$2,000 to $5,000 split with the illustrator
  Royalty—10 percent, 5 percent to the author and 5 percent to the illustrator

Big Books (for author only)
    Flat fee—$250 to $500
    Advance—$0 to $1,000
    Royalty—5 to 8 percent

Computer Books
    Flat fee—$500 to $1,000
    Advance—usually none
    Royalty—3 to 10 percent

Textbooks
    Since individual chapters in most textbooks (through grade twelve)
        are written by different authors and payment depends on so many
        factors such as grade level, length of chapter, research required,
        and content, the rates vary considerably.

    One can expect a flat fee of $500 to $4,000 for a chapter.
    The author (or authors) of the text itself, not the contributing au-
        thors, usually receives an advance and royalties.
    College and university textbooks pay the highest royalties, ranging
        from 18 to 24 percent. They often take two to three years to write
        and another year or more to publish.

    For some miscellaneous contribution to textbooks, you can ex-
pect approximately:

    One page of enrichment materials for a math text—$150 to $200
    Set of ten test items for the instructor—$25 per item or $250 per
        page
    One- to five-page stories for a literature anthology—$200 to $300
    Elementary math text workbook—$800 to $1,000
    Junior high text—$6,000 to $8,000
    One page for a textbook—$50 to $75
    Work text—flat fee range of $2,000 to $6,000 depending on the
        grade level and content

II

The Journey of a Book Manuscript

EVERY BOOK BEGINS IN THE SAME WAY—WITH AN
author—but publishing a book is a long and involved process.
Although it may not directly make you a better writer, it will help
you to understand and appreciate the role of the publishing company. In most cases, the author writes the material, but it is the
editorial staff, illustrator, designer, marketing director, printing
department, and many other members of the publisher's staff who
take the text you have put so much time and effort into and make
it into a market-ready book.

Every publishing house works differently: The staff may be large
or small, everything may be done in-house or outside editors, designers, and illustrators may be used. This chapter will give you
an understanding of what generally takes place from the written
proposal to the finished book.

The following eighteen steps are the way one firm handles books
such as teaching aids, teacher resources, and classroom or curriculum materials in language arts and the sciences.

1. Proposal arrives at the publishing house
2. Author is informed of publisher's interest
3. A cost analysis is prepared by the publisher
4. A contract is sent to the author
5. Author returns the contract
6. Completed manuscript is received at the publishing house
7. An editor evaluates the project and revises as necessary
8. A copyeditor reviews and corrects the manuscript
9. Manuscript is assigned to a designer
10. Marketing and advertising are planned
11. Proofs are sent to the author
12. Artist submits rough art
13. Artwork completed
14. Paste-up or scanned artwork
15. Printing
16. Complimentary copies sent to the author
17. Books sent to the warehouse for storage and distribution
18. Copies sent to reviewers

Publishing House Receives Proposal

Proposals are opened, read, and sorted by an editorial assistant or other staff person. If the material is not suitable for the publishing house, it is placed in the author's SASE and returned. If there is no SASE, it is more than likely discarded.

In larger houses, your proposal may be first read by a reader, in smaller houses by the editor (who may also own the company).

The editorial assistant sends the manuscript to the editor for consideration. He or she will read it carefully and consider if it would fit into the publishing schedule (if it is similar to anything they already have) and compare it to the competition. Sometimes the manuscript is sent to an outside reviewer for evaluation.

If the editor or editorial director decides that the project is good and wants to issue a contract, he or she then discusses it with the publisher.

The author will then be informed of the publisher's interest.

This could take from a few weeks to six months from the time your proposal is sent. Some companies may take even longer, but if you do not hear anything after three months, you should either call or send a letter asking if your proposal is still under consideration. Your good news may come in a short note or letter or by telephone. You will be given the terms such as royalty and advance, and you may be asked for or given a due date for the manuscript.

If you accept, a cost analysis is prepared. It includes the size and number of pages, which helps determine the book's price and the number of copies for the first printing. The cost of producing a book is figured on a per page price and is determined by the publisher. If illustrations are used, the price is higher than a book with text only. The editor or editorial director presents the cost analysis information to the president and finance officer, who sign the offer for the project.

Issuing the Contract

The contract is prepared, and two copies are sent to the author. If the author is working jointly with the illustrator on the project, a contract will be sent to each, and royalties for each will be one-half of the normal percentage paid. If an advance is given, it, too, will be shared fifty/fifty.

After reading the contract carefully, the author returns both copies of the signed and dated contract for the signature of the editorial director and/or publisher or the person responsible. One copy will be returned to the author for his or her own files. If the project is submitted by an agent, he or she also gets a copy of the contract.

More information on contracts is presented in chapter 6, "The Writing Business."

Completed Manuscript Is Received

The contract states the date the finished manuscript is to be submitted. When it is received, an editor evaluates the project. This may be an in-house editor or a free-lance editor.

During this time you may be asked to rewrite certain chapters or other portions of your book, or if it doesn't come up to the planned page count, you may have to write several pages of additional text. The space required for illustrations or photographs may take more or less space than was originally planned. Or, you may be asked to omit chapters or portions of the book if manufacturing estimates indicate need for a trim, in order to price the book competitively.

With my book *The Little Scientist,* I was asked to write several pages of additional activities, because the word count was short for the required pages. Although this was not difficult to do, it did take extra time for which I had not planned. With another book for the same editor, *Science Toolbox,* I was over the planned page number and was asked to cut almost ten pages. This was difficult to handle, as it is never easy to cut out material you have spent so much thought and effort writing. After agonizing over the task and procrastinating as long as possible, I took my manuscript and forced myself to cut, cut, cut!

A copyeditor reviews the manuscript when the editor has finished. The production editor or the copyeditor reads and codes the elements of the book—heads, body text, contents—and special elements, such as part openers, number lists, bulleted lists, or anything else that might be unusual. The manuscript, along with an art list, will be given to the assigned designer.

During this time, marketing is also being planned by the marketing director (who, in very small companies, may also be the editorial director). Market planning takes place throughout the year for all titles scheduled by the company. Book clubs, foreign rights, and any other marketing possibilities will be considered for each book on an individual basis.

Proofs are sent to the author, sometimes simply as a courtesy, but there may be a particular reason why they need to be checked by the author.

Artist and Designer

Deciding on the layout, print size, and margins and creating camera-ready pages are part of the designer's job. In many educational houses, the designer will do this by computer. Books with color illustrations or photos may go through a different process.

In some cases the artist/illustrator may also design the book. If a publisher has an art staff, they may design the book, or they may decide to use an outside designer whom the editor would contact.

The designer uses information from the editor and the coded manuscript as a guide for creating sample pages. Decisions are also made regarding type style, size and weight of paper, column widths, and placement of art.

If free-lance artists are used, they will be assigned the project as soon as a book dummy (a mock-up) is made. The dummy pages that have illustrations are photocopied, and one or more pages will be given to the illustrator. If the author has made any sketches, copies will also be passed on to the illustrator. The illustrator will be given a date when pencil sketches are due. It makes no difference if an illustration is to be completed using conventional means or the computer, it all starts with a pencil sketch. This is also true of art in color. The designer will show the editor or editorial director the pencil sketches along with any comments they may have. The pencil sketches are returned to the designer by the editor with any corrections needed. The illustrator is given the sketch with the corrections noted and asked to do the finished illustrations.

Conventional—Once the manuscript is approved and marked up for typographic design, it is sent to the typesetter (most typesetters today use computerized equipment). Regardless of how they are produced, the first proofs from the typesetter are usually referred to as galleys. The galleys will be read by a proofreader and reviewed by a production editor and, in many cases, by the author. This is the last time the author can make corrections or additions, and they must be kept to a minimum or the author will be charged.

Next comes the page layouts, page proofs, paste-ups, and finally the printing plates.

Computer—The pencil sketch will be scanned. The scanned image will be used with an illustration software program as a basis for producing a finished illustration. The more proficient computer illustrator is capable of producing even more complex color illustrations.

The designer shows the finished illustrations to the editor. If corrections are needed, back the illustrations go to the illustrator.

Conventional—Camera-ready boards have all the type in position. If the illustrations are line art they can be pasted in position. Any special instructions will also be included with the boards. The designer turns the boards over to the publisher who, after checking, turns the boards over to the printer.

Computer—Camera-ready boards on the computer are either laser prints or a disk. If any of the illustrations are produced on the computer, they have been incorporated in position on the pages using the page layout software document. A laser print of the pages, with illustrations in position, may be used as camera-ready art. Illustrations not produced on the computer would be pasted on the laser print if they are line art, or indicated if color.

After the artwork and the pages are completed and approved, the complete package is now ready to be turned over to the printer. The designer and illustrator have now completed their tasks.

Printing Process

Camera-ready art is just that, art that is ready for the camera to shoot. The film is used to make printing plates from which the book is printed. Many printers are using computer disks as a source for making the film. New technology has developed printing presses that can process printing plates directly from computer disks. As these technologies advance and prices drop, the computer disk may be the preferred source for making printer plates. It is less expensive to send a computer disk through a mail service or over a modem than it is to send bulky art boards.

The first printing of your book could be 3,000 to 5,000 copies; resource, craft, and similar books can easily be reprinted and probably will be several times during the year. Curriculum-related books and nonfiction picture books that contain photographs or a large number of illustrations will have a larger first printing, perhaps 8,000 to 12,000, because it is not cost-effective to print these books in small numbers.

The final stages deal with folding, gathering, sewing, trimming, and adding the cover.

Paperbacks such as workbooks, may be bound simply by stapling through the center fold. Then a thick, heavy paper cover is wrapped around the pages and stapled into place. Larger books may be stitched together through the backs or down the sides near the back, or they may be glued at the back and the cover then glued in place. After the cover is secured, the book is trimmed. Some nonfiction, biographies, and other curriculum-related books may have a book jacket added.

After Printing

Six months to a year (or as long as two years) have elapsed since you sent in your completed manuscript. But you now have a book. If it is your first publication—you are now a published author!

Complimentary copies are usually sent to the author soon after they are printed. Often there are delays for various reasons, but if you know the publication date and you don't receive your copies soon after, call your editor. There may be a mix-up of some kind, as it was once for me (someone thought someone else had sent the books).

Usually a number of books have been presold. Your editorial director has shown your book at a sales meeting and a blurb has been given to the reps who are now giving your book a push. It may also have been shown at one or more sales and marketing conventions, or an educational conference, in the form of unbound, folded, and gathered galleys.

Books that have been presold and orders that came in as the result of other advertising will be shipped as soon as possible. If appropriate, copies are sent to reviewers.

Books are sent to the warehouse for storage and for distribution to schools, libraries, and bookstores.

When the company's catalog comes out (once or twice a year) you will receive a copy. If not, ask for one. Your book may also be listed in other catalogs as well. For instance, if your book relates to science, it may appear in catalogs that offer science equipment and resources. For example, a book on insects, science experiments, or learning about science tools such as magnifying glasses, thermometers, or measuring devices might be listed in Nasco, Edmund Scientific, and/or Wards science catalogs.

Since sending your completed manuscript, you, of course, have not been sitting idly by. You have been working on your next book, which will soon be ready to start on its journey!

12

Recycling Your Ideas and Your Research

WHAT CAN YOU DO WITH ALL THE LEFTOVER RE-search material from your book? Don't throw it out, for you have put in many hours of hard work to ferret out that valuable information. Recycle it into another project.

Magazines provide an abundance of opportunities for recycling the material you do not use in your book. Children's magazines—general, religious, educational, and parenting—are possible markets for reusing your research material or for using those new ideas that so often come to you when you are involved in writing a manuscript.

You can write fiction or nonfiction for magazines in your areas of expertise or special interest. Magazines focusing on history, science, space, astronomy, and math as well as other areas of the curriculum all offer opportunities. Whatever you want to write about, you can find a magazine where your topic fits by studying the market.

You may write a magazine article on iceworms, which have been found only in glaciers in Alaska, that will develop into a curriculum-related book on glaciers; or your leftover research from a curriculum-related book, such as my book on crystals, might be the basis for a magazine article on collecting and identifying rocks containing crystals, starting a rock collection, or a puzzle on different kinds of crystals or types of rocks.

The ten pages my editor had me cut from *Science Toolbox* were geared to first through third grade. Earlier, we had talked about possibly doing a science toolbox book for fourth through sixth grades based on the same format. This means I already have ten pages from the first book plus pages of leftover research that I can use by rewriting and directing it toward older children.

Reslant, Rewrite, and Resell

Writing is contagious. Once you start, you will discover that new ideas keep coming to you and new doors keep opening.

Rewrite your material for a different age group, slant it to a different market, update old or existing material by using newly discovered information, reorganize by perhaps writing the facts as a novel or as an alphabet book.

For example, if you write a book on ecology, you may have research material that would get you started on a biography or picture book on Rachel Carson or a similar contributor to the preservation of our environment. First you will need to investigate the market to find out at which publishing companies and at which age level there is no book available.

Maybe your unused material from your nonfiction book or the activities in your research book would fit into an easy-to-read or a Hi-Low, fiction or nonfiction book. Easy-to-read, also called beginner books, are used with preschool and kindergarten children who are ready to read, non–English-reading students, and anyone who has a problem learning to read. Among the easy-to-read publishers are Macmillan (Ready-to-Read), Sesame Street (Start-to-Read), and Greenwillow (Read-Alone). Hi-Low means high interest, low vocabulary, which provides easy reading for slow or reluctant readers. These books are available at different reading levels (elementary through high school), and are also used to teach

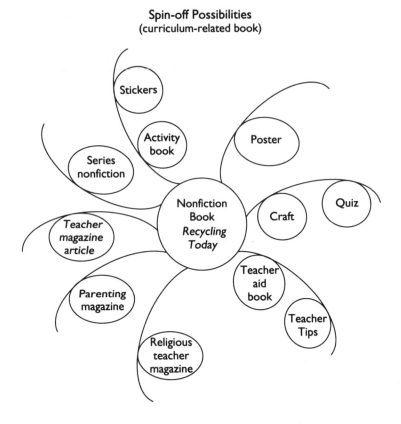

Spin-off Possibilities
(curriculum-related book)

adults to read. For good examples of Hi-Low books, read some of the *Amelia Bedelia* books (series by Peggy Parish) published by Harper Trophy Books.

One needs to be familiar with these books—short sentences, no paragraph indentation, and a ragged-right edge (nonjustified right margin)—before attempting to write them. You will usually find easy-to-reads and Hi-Lows in a special section of the library. Check out as many as possible from different publishing companies, and study them. Publishers have special guidelines that cover vocabulary, sentence length, and other particulars—send for them.

The nineties is called by many the "golden age of children's books." Choose the genre within the children's field where you wish to write, be it fiction or nonfiction. There may be portions within your published book that you could expand on to make it visually oriented and become an information picture book.

If you have written a picture book and your manuscript has been returned several times, reread it carefully—you may find it is more appropriate for a magazine.

I wrote an activity book on Mother Goose and later rewrote some of the rhymes and extended the ideas into matching games and puzzles for a magazine.

Several of my books are science related and I have been able to sell leftover or deleted experiments to magazines. Other material was rewritten and developed into a nature story.

An author friend of mine, while doing research for a book on one of the South American countries for Dillon Press's "Discovering Our Heritage" series, came up with an idea for a craft book based on geography, which sold to a publisher of teacher learning materials. It included projects such as how to make a relief map, a world globe from inflated balloons, and a U.S. map with each state cut from a different fabric. Other spin-offs might be a cultural cook or song book or an article for a teacher's magazine on crafts the world around.

Material from a workbook or curriculum related book on math might possibly work into a counting book; or unused photographs could be the origin of a wordless (contains no text) photo book for preschoolers.

A nonfiction article on camping could be rewritten and slanted to different age groups—first for *Boys' Life* (ages eight to eighteen), next to *Cricket* (ages seven to fourteen) on overnight, backyard camping, and then to *Turtle* for preschoolers on setting up camp in your bedroom.

You may find ways to work material into a filmstrip, play, or reader's theater, or you may develop a table game.

I find snails absolutely fascinating. These creatures have inspired me to create quizzes, nature stories, puzzles, movement activities, nonfiction articles, and rhymes for several magazines, plus items for religious and educational markets based on my research and knowledge of snails alone! Over half of the books I have written contain something about snails. I probably have enough research material for several books, and I can tell you almost anything you care to know about snails. One day, when I find the right slant, I may write an encyclopedia on snails!

The Snowball Effect

It only takes a tiny snowball of an idea to get things rolling. Before you know it, the tiny ball is a giant rolling snowball that just keeps on rolling, rolling, rolling.

My snowball idea was a story that developed out of a storytime with my granddaughter. After having been packed tightly and the edges smoothed, it became a story for *Highlights for Children* magazine.

As my snowball began to pick up more snow, there was a similar story, with a different slant, rolling off to *Ranger Rick Nature Magazine.* These two snowball stories, plus two more and an outline were on a roll to become a ninety-six-page book of cut-as-you-tell stories and rhymes for Pitman Learning, which is now Fearon Teacher Aids. Three small snowflakes fell off the big snowball and each developed into another snowball book for the same publisher. Bits of snow continued to fall off and start new snowball books until one day there were eleven!

But my snowball didn't stop. As it rolled along, a piece broke off and became another snowball, which split in half and became two snowball books for a religious publishing house, Standard Publishers. My now giant snowball and the two smaller ones rolled along picking up more snowy ideas. The two smaller ones continued to pick up snow and grew as stories developed for several religious magazines; the giant snowball split off into several stories for nonreligious, children's magazines.

Have my snowballs stopped rolling? No, they just bumped into another pile of snowball manuscripts I was working on. They are ready to roll again—they just need a little push. Right now, I have no idea where they will roll to next, if they will ever stop rolling, or how big they will become.

Your little snowball of an idea can, like mine, become a giant snowball. But you have to get it started, so give it a push and write and rewrite, and submit and resubmit. Get *your* snowball rolling, and before you know it, you will be on a roll, too!

13

Getting into Children's Magazines

OVER TWO HUNDRED MAGAZINES, BOTH FOR CHIL-
dren and adults, accept *educationally* related stories and articles.
Any form of the written word that children are reading or that is
being read to them is a part of their education.

Options within the children's magazine field are limited only
by the writer's imagination. Magazines are published for preschool
children through the teen or young adult level.

Children's magazines are used in the classroom as a supplement
to a reading book, which also promotes the whole language theory; school libraries stock a variety of magazines; public libraries
allow magazines to be checked out; and parents subscribe to a
number of magazines for their children.

Stories from one to four pages, nonfiction, biographies, celebrity profiles, sports figures, poetry, action rhymes, finger plays,
rebus stories, photo-essay, science experiments, crafts, how-to,
mazes, puzzles, and games are just a few of the opportunities available to you as an author. If you cannot find a way to recycle your

ideas or your research, create new material and submit it to an appropriate magazine.

Rebus stories and puzzles are popular in several magazines, but there is a difference in the type accepted. The two kinds, with some variations, of rebuses are:

1. *True rebus*—words are illustrated with pictures, letters, and symbols (I + picture of a heart + U for "I love you").

2. *Noun-picture rebus*—in the story a picture replaces, or is sometimes placed before or after, each noun (The [picture of a girl] has a [picture of a dog]).

I have sold several rebus stories, rhymes, and puzzles. One rebus story I wrote for *Highlights for Children* was returned, but I was able to rewrite it using only pictures in place of nouns and pictures and sell it to *The Friend* magazine.

Submitting Magazine Material

For most fiction, you don't need to query or even include a cover letter. However, a query letter should be sent for nonfiction articles, unless they are very short or the guidelines ask for the complete manuscript. Some magazine publishers—*Cobblestone, Faces, Calliope*—work on a theme, and the usual procedure is to query with an idea for the theme. You will be sent a theme list when you write for guidelines, but only if you request it.

Magazines are usually copyrighted in their entirety; however, most publishers will give you back the book rights if you have a book contract.

Two publishers, for stories that had originally appeared in their magazines, gave me back the book rights for use in *Paper Stories*. Credit to the magazines was given and a copy of the book was sent to each magazine editor.

Another bonus for the author is that magazine stories and poems are sometimes reprinted in textbooks, reading books, or anthologies. Publishers of supplementary readers usually buy nonexclusive book rights, so your story or poem could possibly be sold to more than one company.

Magazine publishers work six months to a year in advance;

therefore, holiday material for next year should be submitted soon after the holiday. Turnaround time on a manuscript is from one to three months.

As you study magazines and guidelines you will discover certain restrictions apply to some magazines, and that others have a definite focus. For instance, *Highlights for Children* does not accept games or puzzles that require any writing in the magazine, and samples of a completed craft item must be included with the directions; *Ranger Rick* does not want stories with "talking" animals; and *Odyssey* accepts only material that relates to space and astronomy.

Magazines are an excellent vehicle for collecting writing, illustrating, and photo credits. Not only does your item appear in print faster but also you get paid sooner, and less time is required for writing and researching. Writing for magazines is an excellent practice field for authors, and seeing your work in print, along with a tag or byline, will boost your ego and motivate you to keep writing. Every item you have published helps build your credit list.

Magazines, too, can be a springboard to a published book. It was for me. My first story was sold to a children's magazine. This story later became one of the thirty-one stories and rhymes that made up my first book, *Paper Stories.* Shortly after it was published, I used the same format to sell two books to a religious publishing house.

Children's Magazine Markets

Where do you find these magazine markets? Read as many children's magazines as possible. Check out several back issues of a dozen or so magazines from your local library. Read them, study them, write for their guidelines, and submit your material to the appropriate ones.

Writer's Market; Children's Writer's and Illustrator's Market (both published by Writer's Digest Books); and *Writer* magazine (April issue) list juvenile and young adult markets. These market listings include the publisher's address, type of material accepted, need for art, and usually the payment range.

To find out which subjects have been recently covered, consult the *Children's Magazine Guide* published monthly by R. R. Bowker. The magazines indexed by the guide are found inside the front cover of each issue. Most large libraries have a copy.

Children's magazines also need illustrators; some use photographs, especially for the cover. All children's magazines contain some type of art. If you are an illustrator or photographer, query several magazines to find out how to submit your work for review.

Payment for Children's Magazines

Magazine publishers don't pay as well as book publishers, and they do not pay royalties or give advances. However, if the magazine pays on acceptance, you will get paid shortly after being notified of acceptance. You should see your item in print usually within six months.

Read the magazine guidelines carefully. Some publishers pay on acceptance, which means shortly after they inform you of their acceptance; others pay on publication, which means you do not get paid until your story or item is published. This could mean a year, or never. The publisher may inform you that they would like to hold your manuscript and perhaps use it later. If you agree to this and they haven't published it after a reasonable length of time (six months to a year), you should write and ask that it be returned, and then submit it elsewhere.

The amount of payment you can expect varies with each publisher and depends on the length and type of item, but the following is an average:

Fiction—$40 to $500
Nonfiction—$50 to $750
Rebus—$25 to $100
Games and puzzles—$10 to $75
Crafts—$10 to $30
Poems—$5 to $50
Action rhymes—$20 to $80

Average payments for illustrations and photographs can be found in chapter 5.

Don't underestimate the importance of these so-called alternative markets as ways to recycle your ideas and your research. Each of these two hundred or so magazines that accept child-related material is published ten to twelve times a year, and publishers must fill up each page each month (see chapters 14, 15, and 16 for other magazine opportunities). You, as a teacher and/or author, can help fill those empty pages. Magazine editors need your ideas, so reach out beyond the traditional book market and write for them!

An Alphabet of Magazine Article Ideas

The following are topics I have found listed in either current magazine guidelines or in recent issues of a variety of children's magazines. Hundreds of articles, stories, and other items could be written on each topic. To help get you started, here are my ABC's of topics for your potential articles (add your own topics):

A—action rhyme; activities; adventure; animals; antidrug, tobacco, and alcohol; anthropology; art; astronomy

B—biographies, book reviews, birds, boats

C—careers, children, computers, concepts, conservation, contemporary stories, cooking, crafts, creative movement rhymes and activities, crossword puzzles, cultural information

D—dolls, dogs, drawing

E—ecology, education, environment, exercises, experiments

F—fables, fantasy, fairs, feathered animals

G—games, gardening, geography, good manners

H—health, historical fiction, history, hobbies, holidays, how-to, human body, humor

I—illustrations, interviews, insects

J—jazz, jogging, jobs, justice

K—kites, kings, knights, kitchen fun

L—limerick, legends, latitude/longitude

M—marine biology, math games, monuments, museums, music, mysteries, maps, map skills

N—natural science, nature, nursery rhymes, nuclear energy

O—outer space, oyxgen, oysters, ozone, olympics

P—pets, photos, photo features, picture-oriented material, poems, problem solving, profiles, puppetry, puzzles

Q—quizzes, quails, queens

R—rebus, recipes, recycling, retold folk- or tall tales, riddles, romance, reading

S—safety, science, science fiction, sea life, sensory activities, short stories, social science, social issues, songs, sports, spy stories, suspense stories

T—technology, travel, teeth, tongue/taste

U—U.S. history, umbrellas, Uncle Sam

V—vacation time, valentines, vapor

W—wildlife, world history, wars, writing

X—X rays, xylophones

Y—yo-yos, youth cultures, yaks, yodeling, yule log, Yukon Territory

Z—zoo animals, zoos, zoology, zippers

14

Educational Magazines

NOT TO BE OVERLOOKED WITHIN THE EDUCATIONAL writing field is the market offered by educational magazines. These magazines provide opportunities for authors to share their teaching ideas, hints, curriculum suggestions, and opinions.

Teacher aides, assistants, substitute teachers, and parents helping in the classroom can share experiences on how they cope with a certain situation or how to achieve an effective working relationship with teachers and/or students. Educational magazines provide a forum for all kinds of ideas.

For example, aides and assistants who work in the classroom might want to submit an article on a topic such as "Working with a Teacher," or "Is There Room for Both Teachers and Aides in the Classroom?"

Substitute teachers may want to share articles such as, "It's Not Easy to Be a Sub," "Have Sub Kit; Will Travel," or "Problem Kids and the Substitute Teacher."

Professional newsletters for the classroom teacher offer another avenue for writers to consider. Parents might find this an area to extend kudos or to encourage other parents to volunteer in the classroom as a way of finding out what's happening at schools.

There are magazines, tabloids, and newsletters geared to all ages—preschool to college. Subjects for contributors include any material that relates to education. Some magazines focus on one area of the curriculum. *School Arts Magazine, Arts and Activities,* and *Technology & Learning* belong to this category.

Most educational periodicals are published monthly during the school year, often with combined issues in July and August and December and January.

My first publishing experience was an idea for a cooking activity that I sent to *Teacher* magazine (now incorporated into *Instructor* magazine) in 1978. It was a three-page manuscript that I had labored over for months. The editor paid me ten dollars and cut the article to one column, but what a joy (and a surprise) to see my work published in a magazine! My tiny space in one magazine motivated me to keep writing and submitting and, within a few years, selling nearly three hundred magazine items.

The Educational Magazine Genre

Specialty magazines on teaching art, science, math, and computers, as well as magazines that are broad-based such as *Learning* and *Creative Classroom,* are choices open to free-lance authors who are connected in some way with the teaching field.

There are also magazines written especially for teachers and caregivers on the care and nurturing of infants, toddlers, and preschoolers. Among these are *My First Magazine, Lollipops,* and *Pre-K Today.* With so many working mothers in our society, the need for child care has risen rapidly over the past several years. Due to the concern and pressure of parents and child caregivers, these programs have developed into "schools" that instruct by helping young children prepare for learning basic skills, expressing creativity (through art, blocks, and daily living play), and discovering the world around them (in nature, community helpers, and with other cultures), as well as learning to socialize and function in group situations and in a new environment—all topics for authors.

A tabloid is a small newspaper format magazine about half the size of a regular newspaper page and is printed on regular newsprint or glossy paper, which makes the magazine less expensive to produce. However, many of these magazines also accept outside material. Tabloids and newsletters usually require a manuscript to contain a certain number of words and to be typed as a column with the number of characters limited to each line. Produced monthly (usually during the school year), they need new, teacher-tested articles to fill each issue.

The content of a tabloid is similar to glossy-cover magazines in that it may include action rhymes, poems, teacher activities, how-to, and helps for teachers and parents. Examples of this type of publication are *First Teacher* and *The Good Apple Newspaper.*

Regardless of the type or size of an educational magazine, being published in any of them provides you with valuable experiences and builds your writing credits.

Books for the educational market are often reviewed in educational magazines. Writing book reviews may provide yet another opportunity to get in print.

Short items such as poems, fingerplays, activities, art and craft projects, holiday ideas, and other short items not requiring research can be worked on when you have only a short time to devote to writing. Try writing one while waiting at the airport, the doctor's office, or waiting to pick up your children from some activity. Interruptions are not as critical to your train of thought, and the writing requires less concentration than other types of articles.

Writing for Educational Magazines

As with any other genre, a writer needs to become familiar with the publication. Each magazine has its own special need and focus. Except for short items, it is best to query first. Most magazines have guidelines, and generally publishers will send sample copies to prospective contributors. As a courtesy, and to make it easier for the person who answers their stacks of mail, I send along with my SASE an adhesive-backed, self-addressed label and ask for a copy of a back issue (but they usually send the most recent issue).

1. *Feature articles*—The average length for short feature articles is about 200 to 1,000 words; for longer features, 2,000 to 3,500 words. Feature articles run from one to three pages.

2. *Holidays*—Holiday material needs to be submitted at least six months in advance (magazines are planned four to six months in advance), but you will want to start sooner. In case your manuscript is returned you will have time to submit to another publication.

3. *Arts-and-Crafts*—Some publishers may require you to send samples or a photograph of the project. Directions need to be clear and simple enough for the student to make *without* teacher help. There is a strong emphasis on crafts and useful items that can be made from throwaway materials or that promote environmental awareness.

4. *Computer Items*—A variety of articles related to computers are found in several educational magazines. Success stories on using computers or specific software in the classroom, reviews of software programs, or how you have adapted a particular program to an area of study, and teacher-created materials or how to write your own program are all open areas for free-lance submissions. You may have an idea for a new column for one area of the curriculum for each issue throughout the school year.

5. *Plays*—Plays written for educational magazines are usually one-act, one-page plays. Many use a narrator. Few if any props or costumes should be required. Hats, headbands, and hand-held facemasks are often used to identify characters.

6. *Regular Columns*—Although some regular columns are staff written, a good idea will always be considered for a new column. Even if your idea is good, you need to consider if there is (or you can come up with) enough material to sustain the column for ten issues. If you feel your idea would be suitable for a regular column, send in a proposal with an outline for ten to twelve months and two or three sample columns. This will help the editor see that you have thought the proposal through and are able to write the additional columns required.

7. *New Product and Book Reviews*—Reviews of new products and books are sometimes written by the publishing staff; however, if you do not find reviews in magazines you might like to write for,

query the publisher with the idea. Enclose a few sample reviews prepared especially for their magazine.

8. *Library Journals*—As a teacher, school librarian, or media specialist, you may have helpful ideas to share on school libraries: organizing the library and media section, helping students learn about libraries or how to do research, decorating your school library or bulletin board, promoting books innovatively, or making your library a place kids can't stay away from. Library journals such as *Horn Book, Wilson Library Bulletin,* and *Library Journal* all accept free-lance material from writers qualified in the field.

9. *Editorials*—When you find yourself strongly in disagreement with something you've read or heard, consider the possibility of turning your reaction into an article. The article will need to be substantiated with data, quotes, or statistics. Read through several issues of the proposed magazine and the guidelines, and then decide if it can be developed from a professional viewpoint and without exaggeration. If it can, write your editorial.

10. *Writing Fingerplays*—Fingerplays, also called action rhymes, are found in many educational magazines, tabloids, and newsletters. Reading, teacher resource, and poetry books often include this type of rhyme.

Fingerplays and rhymes are an integral part of early childhood programs. Some may be four lines long, others may tell a short story. Regardless of the length, teachers and caregivers, as well as parents, find them to be an excellent tool for teaching concepts to toddlers through kindergarten and even first grade.

Sometimes it is impossible to find the exact rhyme that gets across the concept you want to teach. If this is the case, write your own. Keep it simple (this is the difficult part) with short lines, and use repetition. Relate the content to words and objects that are familiar to children—a mouse, bathtub, or paint brush.

If your endeavors prove to be successful, write down one or two rhymes and send them to an educational magazine publisher. Remember to include the actions and to keep them simple enough for young children to memorize and perform. If the publisher likes one (or both) well enough to publish it in their magazine, you may be able to write a book of fingerplay rhymes. Although there are many good ones on the market, there is always room for a book that has some unique feature.

These rhymes, unlike poetry, are both easy and fun to write. Study finger rhymes you find in magazines, browse through an educational supply store's inventory, or check out fingerplay rhyme books from the library.

You will need to emphasize a rather broad theme in order to come up with enough rhymes to make a book. Movement activities where children repeat the rhymes and do activities based on concepts—big, little, up and down—are popular with both teachers and children. Children of the world, using rhymes that involve other cultures playing, dancing, or working, and animals everywhere, including rhymes and actions about a variety of animals (zoo, farm, and sea animals) might be possibilities for developing finger rhymes into a book.

Fingerplays are used in *Instructor* magazine, *First Teacher,* and in some newsletters and parenting magazines. Several children's magazines also use fingerplays or action rhymes. Books I have written on literature and storytelling have included several fingerplays and rhymes.

11. *Artwork and Photos for Magazines*—If only a small amount of art is used in a newsletter or tabloid (and some magazines), it may be done by staff artists. Photographs are used on covers of tabloids and some newsletters. Magazines use color photos, and tabloids use mostly black-and-white. Query several magazine publishers to see if they are interested in seeing samples from freelancers before you send any of your work. Information on payments for photos and art can be found in chapter 5.

Leftover research material from a book or portions from the book itself can be recycled and/or reslanted for a teacher magazine.

I recently sold an article, "Hats on for Hat Day" (which is, by the way, January 20), to *Learning93* magazine. The idea evolved out of my pattern book on making hats. The article gave suggestions for celebrating the day by making hats from recycled material and ended with having a hat show and a parade. I also suggested to the publisher that they might like to write my editor for permission to reprint some of the patterns or perhaps review the book.

Make It!

Family Activities for Preschoolers

Jean Stangl

Your child will understand the sun's heat as it melts broken color pieces on a paper plate.

"I have a little shadow that goes in and out with me," begins Robert Louis Stevenson's poem, "My Shadow." During these warm, sunny months your preschooler will enjoy playing with her own shadow and making hand shadows against an outdoor wall. You can use pieces of yarn to help her measure the length of her shadow several times during the day. Tape the yarn to a wall and add small paper clocks to show the time of day for each. Discover the time of day when the shadow is the longest.

Look for Stevenson's poem at your local library and read it at family time. Encourage your child to share the fun she had discovering how God's sun created shadows for her.

Science in the Sun

You and your preschooler can play a game of trying to find the warmest (and coolest) spot on a hot day. Compare the warmth by feeling such things as soil or sand, your dog's fur while lying in the sun, a wall facing the sun, the family car sitting in the sun. Explain how heat is *absorbed* by objects that sit in the sun (they get warmer and warmer) for a period of time.

Small pieces of wet cloth, paper, cotton, a sponge, and a shallow pan of water placed on the hot sidewalk presents a visual explanation of *evaporation*.

Fade art is a fun activity that will show the power of the sun. Place sheets of construction paper—red, green and dark blue—in full sun. Set small objects on the papers. Check often under the objects.

Sundial

You and your child can make a simple sundial by using a paper plate anchored to the ground with a pencil. Have your child mark the shadow line on the plate with a crayon at different times of the day.

Sunshine Art

Have your youngster place several colors of broken crayons in a paper plate. Set the plate in the sun and watch what happens to the crayons. When melted, tip the plate to mix colors and create designs.

An aluminum cookie sheet set in the hot sun makes a unique drawing pad. When the pan becomes hot, lay a piece of white paper in the pan and slowly draw on the paper with crayons.

Make colorful designs by placing a piece of wax paper on newspaper set on a hot sidewalk. Grate old crayons onto the wax paper. Place a second sheet on top and let it sit for a few seconds. Then rub your hand over the top sheet to mix the colors. Pull the newspaper to the shade to cool the crayons.

Crayons will melt quickly in the hot sun so remind your preschooler not to leave them outside unattended.

Talk with your preschooler about how the sun helps us, and then ask what she thinks it would be like if there was no sun. You may want to end this "talk" time by thanking God for making the sun. □

Jean Stangl is an author, seminar leader, and an early childhood instructor. She and her husband, Herbert, have three grown children.

Writing for Educational Newsletters

Newsletter publishers accepting free-lance material provide guidelines (many have monthly themes); examples of educational newsletters include *Cottonwood Monthly* for language arts teachers and *Totline Newsletter* for preschool teachers. Classroom activities, games, lessons, songs, science activities, and poetry are some of the ideas one can submit. In the case of themes (holidays, art experiences, and other cultures), you send an outline based on the theme; if accepted, you will receive an assignment to write the article. Items accepted by newsletters include but are not limited to recipes, book reviews, how-to articles, holiday ideas, craft projects, and a variety of short articles.

Locating Markets for Educational Magazines and Newsletters

If you are teaching in a school, you may have access to educational magazines that you can study. Some libraries may carry one or several of the most popular magazines. You may also want to consider subscribing to two or three, as they are seldom found at magazine stands or bookstores. Newsletters for preschool teachers can usually be reviewed through a college early childhood lab school or child care center. *Writer's Market* and the November issue of *Writer* magazine both publish a market list of educational magazines and newsletters.

For an educational magazine and newsletter market list, see the appendix.

Payment for Educational Magazines and Newsletters

Educational magazines pay either on acceptance or publication. Most tabloids and newsletters pay on publication.

Soon after publication, one to three complimentary copies are sent to the author. Additional copies can be purchased at a substantially reduced author's price.

Most of these magazines and tabloids are copyrighted by the

publication; however, book rights will be returned to the author by most publishers. Tabloids, in some cases, retain all rights and then produce booklets compiled of selected material from their publications.

If your concern is to be published for professional advancement, and the monetary reward is irrelevant, you will find college, university, and alumni journals publish papers on a variety of subjects. They usually pay in contributor's copies only, sometimes as many as twenty copies. Still, they are high-quality, often prestigious publications and articles need to be well written and professionally presented.

Children and Science, a highly respected, long-established magazine on science for elementary age children, pays in copies only. However, you do receive a byline and you have your article in print—you are published!

The following payment scale is on average what you can expect. Some tabloids pay the same for each article accepted, and along with newsletters payment will generally be somewhat less than for magazines.

Short articles—$100 to $300
Feature articles—$125 to $500
Art and craft projects—$15 to $75
Fingerplays and action rhymes—$15 to $100
Plays—$40 to $150
Poems—$15 to $50
Reviews—$20 to $100
Tabloids—$50 to $125
Newsletters—$10 to $50

For a list of teacher and educational associations and organizations, see the appendix.

15

Parenting Magazines and Newsletters

MAGAZINES AND NEWSLETTERS THAT FOCUS ON PARenting or cover topics of interest to parents are other markets where teachers and authors can submit educational manuscripts. Traditional women's magazines like *Woman's Day* and *Family Circle* and those specifically for seniors such as *Alive* usually contain one or more articles or items relating to children and their education.

Before you submit material to magazines or newsletters, know the age level covered by the publication. A magazine may be interested only in educational articles for infants and toddlers or for preschool to grade three.

Articles relating to parenting or the education of children, as well as special features, book reviews, regular columns, or a kids' page are a few of the choices open to the free-lance author.

Parents' Magazines

Family Fun, a popular new magazine, published by Disney, accepts read-aloud stories and is especially interested in articles dealing with families and activities the whole family can enjoy.

Working Mother magazine has published articles on music and dance, latch-key kids, and why preschoolers need school.

Parents magazine uses articles on the development and behavior of children preschool through adolescence, baby care and early childhood, and short items used for fillers.

Parent's Digest, published three times a year by *Ladies' Home Journal,* accepts queries for articles dealing with children, education, and parenting.

Helping your child plan for school; the teacher, the parent, and the child; or an article on the danger to the young child who wears boots or thongs to schools (climbing apparatus and running, jumping, and hopping activities) are ideas that could be considered for these magazines.

Magazines for older adults or seniors often contain stories about children and grandparents and articles and tips on grandparenting. How to grow your own food, how grandparents can encourage kids to read, and teaching grandchildren math and science at the workbench or in the kitchen are possible topics.

Lady's Circle uses articles on bringing up children; *Baby Talk* would be interested in articles on the importance of early language input for infants or the development of language; for *Expectant Mother* you might slant an article on decorating the nursery to stimulate early sensory awareness; or an article on the effect of poor nutrition on the ability of children to concentrate in the classroom might be appropriate for a family health magazine.

Local magazines, tabloids, or newspapers are often looking for family entertainment, travel, or interesting nearby places to visit. If you have an interest in local museums, art, or historical houses or places, you might develop your ideas into articles that could be developed over several issues or that could possibly work into a regular column. Related books for reading, illustrated maps, and historical information would be a way for you as a teacher to involve young people as well as their families in educational activities.

Newsletters for Parents

Newsletters directed to parents, usually those with young children, often accept free-lance submissions. However, some are based on themes, and all articles and items must relate to the theme. Check with your local library or a child care director to see if there is a regional parenting newsletter published in your area. Many major cities publish parenting newsletters, such as *L. A. Parent, Metrokids Magazine* (Philadelphia), *Chicago Parent,* and *Parents' Press* (Berkeley, California).

Parenting newsletters contain articles, tips, and help on parental guidance as well as material on language and speech, life with books, and a child's first day of school. Newsletters for parents of gifted children might be interested in topics about the gifted child in the classroom, identifying the gifted within the culturally diversified classroom, or working with your gifted child's teacher.

Ideas for making your own snack, kids need a hobby, starting a collection, how-to make it or do it, or keeping a journal are possibilities for short articles.

Games and puzzles such as those that focus on developing right and left, help kids learn to spell, or require sequencing or logical thinking skills are often used in newsletters for parents (see the appendix for a listing of newsletter publishers).

Submitting to Parent Publications

Magazines and newsletters may be published monthly, bimonthly, or quarterly. These publications usually work four to six months in advance; however, quarterly publications and those with themes may plan a year in advance. You should not make multiple submissions to any of them. However, some publishers buy only first rights, which means that after your article is published, you can submit the same article to another publication that buys second rights. Second rights would be typed under the word count on the first page.

You will want to read several back issues in order to get the feel of the publication. In most cases, you should send a query, unless the guidelines ask for the complete manuscript. Games, puzzles, recipes, and other short items usually do not require a query letter, unless they are theme related.

Newspaper Articles

Although not all newspaper publishers will pay for your first article, there are many possibilities for educationally based submissions. After you write a few items for free, your chances will be better for writing a regular column or feature for pay, especially with smaller newspapers.

You can submit simultaneous articles to several newspapers as long as the readership does not overlap. An example would be sending the same article to the *Los Angeles Times,* a newspaper in San Diego and another in San Francisco, or to a newspaper in another state. Small-town or regional newspapers offer yet another market where you can often sell the same article to three or four different ones if you inform the publishers you are doing so.

Don't overlook the free, weekly local tabloids or newspapers found in the give-away racks at local markets or drugstores, or that are tossed on your doorstep. Check the racks in your area. Sending in a few gratis articles at first may possibly result in a regular, paid column even from free publications, as they are supported by advertising. These publications often have a small staff and are anxious to receive free-lance queries or submissions. *Long Island Parenting News,* a free community newspaper, *buys* articles on child care, schools and camps, and back to school, as well as fillers and photographs.

Popular regular columns often lead to syndication (you sell your articles to a syndicate that pays you for the right to publish your work in several different newspapers). Self-syndicating your column is another alternative you may wish to consider. Syndicated columns are written far in advance and you must prove that you can continue to provide daily, weekly, or monthly columns as required. (Chapters from your book could possibly become a column.)

Suggested topics for newspaper articles or columns might be book selections for kids or parents; gardening with kids; questions and answers on behavior, reading, or speech; places of interest in your local area; or family picnic sites.

Newspapers often have articles on local school news. In some instances they may be written by students, but if your newspaper does not carry such a feature, propose one to the editor. If you can provide quality photographs, mentions this; if not, the newspaper will generally provide a photographer.

Writing letters to the editor is a good way to hone your writing skills as well as express your opinion. Larger newspapers also have an Op-Ed page, which appears opposite the editor's column, for which you may wish to write an editorial relating to schools or education. Payment is usually made for articles used in the Op-Ed section.

For names and addresses of newspapers, check the Yellow Pages of telephone directories, which can usually be found in your library along with *Writer's & Photographer's Guide to Newspaper Markets* by Joan and Ronald Long. Also look for *How to Make Money in Newspaper Syndication* and *Guide to Newspaper Syndication,* both by Susan Lane.

Photographs and Artwork for Parenting Publications

Most magazines and some newsletters may have their own art and photo staff; however, one can always inquire about the possibilities of contributing. Magazines and newsletters look for unique cover photographs, and a newspaper editor may be particularly interested if you have captured an on-site photograph that staff photographers didn't.

Before sending photographs to magazines, newsletters, and local newspapers, call the editor of the publication and discuss the project (see chapter 5 for submitting photographs).

Sources for Parenting Publications

Your local library is the best and least expensive source for magazines. Check out several back issues of ones that interest you, or purchase your own copies to have for long-term reference. Inside the cover is a column referred to as the masthead, which contains the editor's name and the address of the publication. Their guidelines are free for an SASE, and some may send sample copies.

Some libraries also carry parenting newsletters, or you may

write for a sample copy and guidelines. If you can't find copies of a particular newsletter, you may want to subscribe to the newsletter for a short period.

The *Writer's Market* and *Writer* magazine (June issue) contain listings of parenting publications (see the appendix for a listing of parenting magazines and newsletters).

Payment for Parenting Publications

Magazines may pay either on acceptance or after publication. With adult-type magazines, assignments are usually given based on a query letter. The author is then given the go-ahead to write and submit the article. A kill fee, a payment made if the publisher decides not to use the article, is part of the contract issued by many of the more popular or well-established magazines.

Payments vary and frequently it is the policy to discuss the fee and deadline with the author at the time the assignment is made. Payment is usually higher for assigned articles. After publication, most publishers send complimentary copies to the author.

Parenting magazines
> Short items—to 250 words, $10 to $100
> Longer articles—1,500 to 3,000 words, $750 to $2,000 or
> $.10 to $.25 per word

Parenting newsletters
> Short items—$8 to $25. More than one item can usually be sent for
> each issue.
> Longer articles—$50 to $100

Newspapers—articles are usually considered on an individual basis. Regular contributors are paid more. Payment also varies according to the newspaper's size and prestige.

> Sample payments—$0 to $50 (smaller)
> $10 to $150
> $.25 to $2 a column inch

16

Writing for the Religious Educational Market

With the growth and expansion of church-related schools and home teaching programs, the religious materials market is thriving and offers a wide variety of opportunities for authors who wish to pursue this specialized genre. Since religious publishers do not or cannot pay as well as other publishers, many writers enter this field because they enjoy nurturing the faith of youngsters and sharing educationally related ideas with parents and teachers. Altruistic or religious motivations aside, this is a productive way to get published.

Curriculum materials for day school and Sunday school, fiction and nonfiction books, magazines for children, teachers, and parents, and audiovisual materials are some of the options for authors.

Publishing houses affiliated with denominations need a constant supply of materials to supplement ongoing religious studies for children.

Sunday school is not just a random study of scripture and religious beliefs. According to Wesley Tracy, who teaches classes on writing Christian publications and is a former editor of *Teens Today,* various denominations and publishers develop precise educational outlines for all age groups, and millions of dollars are spent on developing Sunday school curricula.

Along with guidelines, publishers may also have theme lists, editorial calendars, curriculum charts, or tip sheets to define their particular needs.

Because it is a religious publication does not always mean it is all scriptural or biblical, although some are. Many include stories about everyday life, character building, and nature, as well as concepts, poetry, and general information articles.

For older children, articles and stories that deal with problem solving, peer pressures, family relationships, and social issues are in demand. Often in fiction, a subtle moral or lesson is interwoven with the character, but editors warn authors about being "preachy."

However, some publishers do want articles, stories, and puzzles slanted to Catholic doctrine, Jewish life, or with a Protestant Christian emphasis.

Each denomination has its own particular needs and emphasis. Standard Publishing, Gospel Light Press, and David C. Cook Publishing Company are among the noteworthy nondenominational publishers; Augsburg, Broadman, Cokesbury, and Paulist Press are examples of reputable publishers affiliated with specific denominations.

When quoting biblical scripture, keep in mind that the King James Version of the Bible is in public domain and can be used freely; however, all new and revised versions are under copyright and you must receive permission from the publisher to use more than the "fair use" (fifty words) from any recent version. Whether fair use or with granted permission, you should always include a credit line when quoting from any Bible version other than the King James.

Religious education magazines may be published monthly, bimonthly, or quarterly. Quarterly magazines plan issues up to two years in advance, and holiday material will be due six to twelve months in advance.

Write for and read the guidelines for religious publications carefully as most do not accept material on Santa Claus, the Easter

Bunny, or Halloween. Smaller magazines may not accept material during June, July, and August.

Some small denominational magazines may not be copyrighted. If this is the case, in order to keep your material from going into public domain once it is published, you should add at the bottom of *each* page a small "c" in a circle, your name, and the date. (It is not necessary to register your work with the U.S. Copyright Office.)

Religious Curriculum Material

Most curriculum material is written on assignment. If you have an interest in writing material for Sunday school, church programs, or weekday programs, write the publishing house of your choice asking for guidelines, curriculum outlines, or other information available to authors. Send a bio and/or information on your background and belief, and the age level for which you wish to write.

All editors ask that you know their market and write to the publication's needs. The usual procedure is for the publisher to send a questionnaire, which, when returned, will be kept on file to use for making assignments. You may be asked to do a sample project such as a story, short take-home paper, or craft project before an assignment is given.

Writing curriculum material will help you gain experience in a variety of writing areas, and these will increase your credits and your credibility as a writer.

Take-home papers were devised by religious educators as a between-Sundays bridge-building strategy, which means publishers must come up with new material for each week. These papers are usually related to the Sunday school curriculum or are based on a theme. The contents for a take-home paper for younger children might include a short story and an activity such as dot-to-dot, coloring picture, or a fingerplay or action rhyme. For older children, a longer story or a nonfiction article, along with a Bible quiz, logical thinking puzzle, a craft project, or a recipe might make up the take-home paper. These small publications may or may not contain related scriptural verses or daily Bible readings.

Authors usually write one or more items for each paper, or a "set," such as a set of ten stories.

Curriculum material written on assignment means it is work for hire because royalties and advances are not given for this type of writing. But once you complete a project, you will no doubt continue to receive assignments.

I have written take-home papers, teaching units, craft projects, and short stories under a work for hire agreement. For a craft book, I wrote the section for four- and five-year-olds for a flat fee. Although my name did not appear on the cover, it was listed on the inside cover as a contributor.

Books of resources for religious teachers, bulletin board pattern books, and complete craft books often do pay a royalty. Seldom is an advance given except for picture books, middle grade, and young adult novels. However, one can sometimes negotiate for a royalty contract.

After the publication—by a secular firm—of my cut-out book, *Paper Stories,* I contacted my editor, who gave me permission to write a similar book using Bible stories. Since my publisher did not publish religious material, the book would not be competing against their market. I sent a query, two sample stories with cut-outs, and an outline for ten stories to an independent religious publisher. I was called by the acquisition editor, who informed me of the publisher's desire to offer a contract if I was willing to write two books—one using Old Testament stories and another using New Testament stories. I agreed and was told their policy was a flat fee payment. I quickly replied that I was hoping for a royalty basis, because I felt I could help promote the book on the West Coast where I periodically present workshops and seminars at three different religious denominational conferences. I later received a royalty contract, and at the end of the first six-month royalty period, my check was more than the original flat fee offer.

Religious Teachers' Magazines

Teacher magazines are used in both church schools and home teaching programs. They may be either denominational or non-

Church Take-home Paper

Sample of a four-page, take-home religious publication for use with two- and three-year-olds.

page 1

Bible verse   Bible reference
illustration
poem, rhyme, or rebus

page 2

illustration
short story

page 3

easy craft—color, cut and paste, or color and fold

page 4

page for parents telling how to use the paper, using the lesson as a "together time" for child and parents, and how to relate daily experiences to the lesson

denominational. Among the items accepted are feature articles on school problems, discipline, dealing with parents, and teaching units, which all usually require a query and an overview or synopsis.

Fiction and short items, sometimes referred to as fillers, are submitted as is. Fillers include poems, games, puzzles, and short teaching tips. Fingerplays and action rhymes, plays, worship programs, writing for regular columns, or proposing a new column are other possibilities.

Evangelizing Today's Child (nondenominational) publishes unsolicited articles helpful to Sunday school teachers and Christian education leaders, and various fillers.

Today's Catholic Teacher publishes teaching ideas, curriculum-related material, and articles teachers can use in the classroom.

Home teaching magazines are published for parents who support the concept of home schooling and want to take a direct involvement approach in the education of their children.

Examples of these magazines are *Home Education Magazine,* which looks for articles on how-to, testing, accountability, resources, and working with the public schools, and *Christian Home & School,* which publishes articles on parenting, school life, and issues that affect the home and school.

Religious Parenting Magazines

Religious parenting magazines focus on relationships between children and parents, siblings, and other relatives. Any article relating to child development, school, reading, math, and science are possibilities for this market. Since most articles are nonfiction, guidelines usually ask for a query with an outline and/or a synopsis or overview.

On the basis of a letter requesting guidelines and a bio stating my experience and credits, I was given a contract to write a regular column for a quarterly magazine for parents. I wrote this one-page article on "things to make and do with your preschooler" for over three years.

Queries for articles on all areas of parenting are accepted by *Today's Christian Woman and Christian Parenting Today.*

Christmas, the Annual of Christmas Literature and Art published by Augsburg Fortress focuses on family-oriented Christmas articles, stories, art, and music.

St. Anthony Messenger, a monthly magazine for Catholic families, uses articles on problems dealing with parenting and on personal growth.

It is just as important in the religious field as in any other to write for and study the publisher's guidelines. Some publications such as *Living With Preschoolers* (Southern Baptist Sunday School Board) require manuscripts to be written in a column format using a limited number of characters per line and a maximum line length so the article and illustrations will fit on one page.

Shortly after sending in a query, I received a telephone call from

Activities for Kindergarten and Beyond

MATH

ALL SORTS OF SOCKS

My kindergartners were surprised and delighted one morning when I hauled out a huge laundry basket brimming with socks. During center time, the children sorted the socks into pairs and then classified the pairs into color and size categories. The children even practiced small motor skills as they taught each other

sock-folding techniques they had learned at home.

ANNETTE THORNTON
Collins, Mississippi

LANGUAGE ARTS & MOVEMENT

SPRINGTIME POETRY

Read this poem as your students pretend to munch, clump, squish, and thump their way across the the earth!

A Dinosaur
I'd like to be a dinosaur,
Who lived long, long ago.
Then I could go munch-munch. Munch-
munch. (pretend to bite and chew)
And eat the leaves down low. (bend down
and keep chewing)
I'd like to be a dinosaur,
Who lived long, long ago.
Then I could go clump-clump. Clump-
clump. (stamp feet)
And move my head just so. (move head
about)
I'd like to be a dinosaur,
Who lived long, long ago.

Then I could go squish-squish. Squish-
squish (move feet on floor in tiny circles)
And kick mud with my toe. (kick foot
behind you)
I'd like to be a dinosaur,
Who lived long, long ago.
Then I could go thump-thump. Thump-
thump. (place palms together behind
you and move arms like a tail)
And 'round and 'round I'd go.
I'd like to be a dinosaur,
Who lived long, long ago
Then I could go munch, clump, squish,
thump. (repeat actions)
And have great fun, you know. (smile
brightly)

JEAN STANGL
Camarillo, California

Share this springtime poem with your group and then have fun thinking up more animal antics to add to the list!

The Naming Game
Oh, a butterfly flies
And a grasshopper hops,
And a snake snakes along on his belly;
And a woodpecker pecks
And a hummingbird hums
And a jellyfish floats in his jelly.
Oh, a tumbleweed tumbles,
An antelope lopes,
And a thunderstorm thunders its name;
And a duck ducks for food,
And a bluebird is blue—
What names can you add to this game?

EDITH E. CUTTING
Johnson City, New York

ARTS & CRAFTS

A POCKETFUL OF ART

Here's an instant art project designed to bring fresh perspective to everyday objects. Have children dig into their pockets and backpacks to retrieve common items, such as pencils, baseball cards, coins, barrettes, and so on. Instruct children to place the items on paper and move them into unusual arrangements (upside down, sideways, overlapping). Then have children trace around the object arrangements, remove the objects, and complete the designs with markers or crayons. Experiment with the technique by tracing objects one at a time, then using one color to define each object.

ROSALIE MORGAN
Smyrna, Georgia

BUTTON-DOWN ART

For the following activity you'll need an assortment of colorful buttons (I got mine for free from a shirt factory), crayons, and oaktag. First, have children draw sim-

ple designs or pictures on cardboard or oaktag. To add dimension to their drawings, encourage kids to select and glue buttons onto their designs. If you have enough supplies, you can invite the children to complete the entire picture with buttons or incorporate cloth scraps into their designs.

ROSALIE MORGAN
Smyrna, Georgia

the editor of a Christian family magazine giving me the go-ahead to write an article—a review of religious magazines for teenagers. In doing my research, I discovered I could write a similar article for another parents' magazine and slant it toward giving magazine subscriptions as holiday gifts for younger children. With additional research and finding a new slant, I may be able to review secular children's magazines for a nonreligious magazine or a newspaper.

Other Religious Markets

Alternative markets in the religious educational field include fiction and nonfiction books, folk literature, children's magazines, and teen and college magazines.

More children's books are being published by religious publishing houses than ever before. Religious picture books, middle-grade fiction, and religious versions of fairy tales are now being sold in children's book stores, chain stores, and even grocery markets (Happy Day Books, thirty-two-page picture books on a variety of topics and published by Standard Publishers, is one example).

Children's books may be scriptural in nature and based on biblical stories such as the Creation, the nativity, or the Resurrection; stories about biblical characters; or present-day church leaders, missionaries, or people who have in some way made important contributions to religion. However, since most of these topics have been covered many times, today's authors must find new ways to present this "old" material.

Concordia Publishing House has a series of paperbacks, thirty-two-page books all written in rhyme. According to *Library World,* a magazine for church libraries, these Arch Books are the best-selling children's books in the religious field.

Rewriting folk literature—If you enjoy folk literature, you may be able to revise, rewrite, or find a unique way to present this public domain literature to a religious publishing house as others have done. For example, in the timeless tradition of *This Is the House That Jack Built,* Carol Wedeve's *The Christmas Crib That Zack*

Built (Abingdon) is based on the nativity story. *Humpty Dumpty Together Tales* by Marjorie Decker uses folktales and nursery rhymes as the basis for her book. David C. Cook publishes retold fables and tales with a spiritual message added.

Most book publishers' guidelines state one should submit the entire manuscript for picture books; for nonfiction (except picture books), middle-grade, and teen novels, send an outline and two or three sample chapters.

In children's religious magazines, as with books, some stories may be biblical in nature; however, many are everyday-type stories about families, sharing, sibling rivalry, taking turns, pets, and problem solving.

Since there is little crossover between the readership of denominational magazines (readers of magazines by a Baptist publisher are not likely to be reading magazines by Catholic or Presbyterian publishers) publishers will usually accept simultaneous submissions, or you can sell second or third rights to the story or article after publication. If you send the same item to more than one publisher, you should advise each editor. Although religious magazines pay less than most general audience magazines, by selling the same story or article to several different denominations, the overall remuneration can be just as high or higher. Articles or stories with a particular denominational emphasis can, in some cases, be rewritten and slanted to the doctrine of another denomination.

With nonfiction, such as a nature or travel item, you may also be able to rewrite the article for a secular children's magazine.

Don't overlook the need of religious magazines, both adults' and children's, for short items or fillers.

Sources for Religious Publishers

Familiarize yourself with the publishers that are of interest to you. If possible, visit the education director of a denomination for which you wish to write and ask to browse through or borrow copies of materials to study. A good way to gain firsthand knowledge of material in this area is to volunteer to assist in a children's class, and then later ask the teacher if you can try out your ideas.

Many churches maintain libraries for use by their members. Church librarians are excellent sources of information about reading tastes and available religious publications. They can also inform you of any local writers or writers' organizations. Not only are church librarians knowledgeable about church literature but they also are often writers themselves. Two major church library associations are: Lutheran Church Library Association, 122 W. Franklin, Minneapolis, MN 55404 and Evangelical Church Library Association, P.O. Box 353, Glen Ellyn, IL 60138. Their newsletters cover new book reviews.

Browsing the Christian bookstores and talking with the manager or salesperson is an excellent way of finding out about material being used in schools and Sunday school programs, and which teacher resources, family and parenting magazines, and children's books are the most popular. Be sure to jot down titles and publishers for your files. When you decide on the publishers whom you may want to write for, send for their authors' guidelines and for their catalogs.

When I was developing a Bible school unit, I asked permission to sponsor a ten-day Bible school for four- and five-year-olds at my church (as we did not have a program that summer) to try out my material. I made notes on the children's responses and on the activities that did and did not work. Then after each session I was able to revise and improve my material.

Some religious parenting and teacher magazines can be found in religious bookstores or church libraries. You can also ask the publisher for a sample copy, or for a better overview of the editor's needs, subscribe to the magazine.

Ask pastors or youth leaders about church and church school conferences in your area. If possible, plan to attend and take advantage of the expertise of the publishing house's representative staffing the booth, check through the displays, and pick up catalogs for later study.

The Association of Christian Schools International (ACSI), the Religious Education Congress (Catholic), and the Lutheran Education Association (LEA) hold annual regional conferences (see appendix for addresses). Check with the church school office of the denomination that interests you for conference information.

Both the *Writer's Market* and *Children's Writer's and Illustrator's Market* contain limited listings for religious book and magazine publishers. The December issue of *Writer* magazine lists religious magazine markets.

Religious Writers Marketplace by William H. Gentz (Abingdon Press) gives in-depth information on religious book and magazine markets.

Christian Writers Fellowship International is a Christian writers organization you may wish to consider joining. Write to P.O. Box 730, DeLand, Fl 32721–0730 for information. They provide members with a comprehensive market list, newsletter, and other valuable resources.

Writers should study the major catalogs for Sunday school teachers available from such publishers as Broadman, Cokesbury, and Southern Baptist (see the appendix for a listing of religious markets).

Illustrating Religious Materials

There are many opportunities for illustrators and photographers in the religious market. Many publishers review packages—manuscript and art—for books, magazines, and curriculum materials, as well as review samples of artwork for future assignments.

Larger publishing houses, such as Standard Publishers and David C. Cook Publishing Company, produce posters, teaching pictures, room decorations, bulletin board and mobile kits, and award certificates that require artwork. Companies that publish picture books use illustrators. Concordia Publishing House reviews artwork for future assignments, and Jewish Lights Publishers ask that you query with a résumé and samples.

Photographs are used for illustrating picture books and for magazine covers—either color or black-and-white prints. Inside magazine photographs are usually black-and-white.

For information on submitting art or photographs, query the publisher of your choice.

Payment for Religious Materials

Payment varies considerably within this market. Denominational publishers tend to pay somewhat less than independent publishing houses. Royalties are paid on most books. However, payment for books and curriculum material is often discussed with the author at the time the assignment or contract is given and many factors such as age level, length, and research required will determine the amount paid. Teen magazines tend to pay more for articles, illustrations, and photgraphs than do children's magazines.

Curriculum materials (flat fee)
  Take-home papers—$7 to $15 a story (usually in a set of ten)
  Teaching units—$30 to $100
  Crafts—$10 to $20 each

Resource books
  Flat fee—$200 to $350
  Royalty—3 to 10 percent

Children's books
  Picture books—5 percent to the author, 5 percent to the illustrator
  Middle grade—8 to 10 percent
  Teen—6 to 8 percent

Teacher's magazines
  Articles—$.06 to $.15 per word to $50 to $450 per article
  Fillers—$25 to $60

Parenting magazines
  Articles—$75 to $350
  Column—$25 to $75
  Fillers—$5 to $25
  Poetry—$5 to $25

Children's magazines
  Articles—$.05 per word to $35 to $125 per article
  Fillers—$2 to $15

Teen magazines

    Articles—$.02 to $.04 per word to $35 to $350 per article

    Fillers—$15 to $25

Illustrations

    Color cover—$150 to $600

    Black-and-white cover—$50 to $100

    Inside, black-and-white—$35 to $100

Photographs

    Black-and-white—$15 to $150

    Color cover—$35 to $200

17

Educational Writing: Make It Your Business

WRITING FOR PROFIT, WHICH I AM SURE IS YOUR goal, is a business; therefore, you must follow certain business practices. Although it is not the most enjoyable task and it takes time away from your writing, record keeping is a necessity.

Setting up and maintaining a well-organized record and filing system is almost as important as writing itself. It is imperative that you keep complete and orderly records for two reasons, one for yourself and one for tax purposes—this means keeping track of your work flow and keeping track of your cash flow.

Once you have been published, no doubt the time will come when you will be working on three, four, or even more projects at once. It is also possible that someone forgets to pay you, especially if you are doing a number of work for hire projects where you may not get paid immediately. You need to know if and when you were paid.

For your records, always keep all notes, drafts, research, records of telephone calls, and copies of everything you send, what you send, where, to whom, and when. All correspondence you receive, including rejection slips, should be dated and filed, and if you should ever be audited by the Internal Revenue Service, you can prove that you are writing and sending out proposals and manuscripts with the expectation of getting published and making money (even if you do not sell right away) and not just writing as a hobby.

Records for Yourself

Pay by check whenever possible and keep all receipts and invoices. If the receipt does not tell what the purchase is for, write it on the receipt—photocopies, notepads, file cabinet, and so on. It is also important to keep all bank statements and canceled checks.

You do not need to be a certified bookkeeper or an accountant to keep financial records. Check with an office supply or stationery store and ask a knowledgeable salesclerk to explain the different types of ledgers to you. Purchase a bound ledger or a tablet of ledger paper. A six-column ledger, which sells from $5 to $10, will provide space for itemizing business expenses by IRS categories. Office supplies, car expenses, conferences, and phone bills are some of their major listings. Computer printouts, if they include an income statement, are acceptable to both tax accountants and the IRS. Of course, *all* receipts and income records must be kept. An updated printout provides quick reference information.

I list income as I receive it, but clip all my receipts together, and post books at the end of each month to show total income and expenses. This is an easy, efficient method to use and is not very time-consuming; however, another method may work best for you.

You may want to consider opening a separate bank account for your writing business or, as I have, an account at a different local bank other than the one where I do my personal banking. This came about because of a mix-up in deposits at the bank where I had both accounts.

Here are a few tips to help increase the productivity and profitability of your writing efforts.

Buying Supplies in Bulk

Buying in bulk saves money and time. As soon as you start your second book or even your second article, you are probably "hooked" on writing so now is the time to stock up on office supplies. Buy your stamps by the roll, paper by the ream or box, envelopes (both #10 and 9 × 12) and manila folders by the box, pencils by the dozen, and any other items you can in large quantities. Discount office supply stores usually offer the best prices for supplies purchased in bulk. If this seems like too big an investment, perhaps you and a friend could go together and save on your supplies.

Keeping Track of Your Manuscripts, Queries, and Proposals

If you have only one proposal, query, or manuscript out, no doubt you know the date it was sent, the publishing company (even the address), and the editor's name, but when you have several of each of these circulating among different publishers and you are busy writing, it won't be as easy to recall dates and publishers. However, this is information that needs to be readily available so you will know where your manuscripts and queries are at all times and how long they have been out.

There is certainly more than one way to set up an efficient system for keeping track of your submissions, and everyone must find the one that works best for their particular situation. Here is what works for me.

Books—Each book query, proposal, and manuscript is kept along with all related information and correspondence in a manila folder in an alphabetized filing cabinet (for more on filing, see chapter 3 under "A Place to Write").

All complete, circulating manuscripts are assigned a letter—A, B, C, and so on. I vertical-rule a sheet of lined notebook paper into columns. At the top I list each manuscript and next to it the designated letter. Down the left-hand side of the page I list publishers who publish the kind of material I write. When the manuscript goes out, I list the letter in the column opposite the publisher. Above the letter I write the date. If it is returned, I draw a line through the letter and add the letter opposite the next publisher I have decided on for this manuscript. Each time it goes out and is returned, I add the publisher's name and the "out" and "in" dates to the publisher's list page inside the manila folder for that book. It is then replaced in the appropriate file. This, too, can be easily done on the computer; however, you may want to print out a copy for quick reference.

Guidelines and Catalog Files—I file guidelines in manila folders under categories such as supplemental book publishers, educational book publishers, children's magazines, educational magazines, and religious publishers.

Publishers' catalogs are filed together alphabetically in a cardboard file box; sample magazines are filed in a separate box. New catalogs replace the old ones *after* I have studied them. These file boxes are kept on shelves in my office closet and can be slid out as I need them.

Magazines—My magazine manuscripts are kept in the same type of manila folder as book manuscripts, only in a separate file drawer. I list all the magazines, addresses, and editors' names that I normally sell to on separate 3 × 5 index cards. The title of the manuscript and the mailing date are written on the top of the card and filed in a recipe box with alphabetical dividers (see sample). I can look at my file and tell you every magazine publisher I have submitted to, the manuscripts I have sent, and the date the manuscript went out and was returned. My records also readily tell me how many times each magazine item (nearly three hundred sold) was sent out, who it was sent to, who it was sold to, and the

Magazine Record File Card

Highlights for Children
803 Church Street, Honesdale, PA 18431

title	out	return/sold	paid
Book Rebus Titles	9-15-91	12-2-91	40.00
Alligators	9-20-92	10-21-92	—
Safe in the Storm	10-31-92	11-12-92	135.00
Sea Shell Share	4-12-93	5-27-93	—

amount of the check, and I can tell how many items I have sent and sold to each publisher for whom I have written.

Records for Tax Purposes

Publishers do not withhold state or federal tax from your payments, advances, or royalties; therefore, you are responsible for keeping a record of your writing income and declaring it for tax purposes at the appropriate time.

The IRS does not care how many manuscripts you have circulating; however, they do care how much money you make from the manuscripts you sell and they want to know the *exact* amount.

All income, no matter how small, must be recorded. If you are in a tax bracket where you pay estimated taxes, your payments may increase due to your writing income.

If a publisher pays you over $600 in a calendar year, the firm will report this income to both the federal government and your state tax collector, and the information will be sent to you on Form 1099.

If you live in a state that taxes income, you must also file state income tax.

Self-employment taxes must also be filed if you net over $400 during the calendar year. This makes you eligible for or adds to your Social Security. See IRS publication 505, "Self-Employment Tax," and use schedule SE for filing.

Even if you do not figure your own taxes, you should obtain the following free publications from your local IRS office. Some banks and libraries may also carry tax forms.

Publication 334, "Tax Guide for Small Business," contains a filled-out, sample copy of tax Schedule C, Profit or Loss from Business form.

Publication 587, "Business Use of Your Home," contains information on who is eligible, using your home, home expenses, and other information you need to know if you declare your home as your place of business.

Tax Deductions

Any expenditure you make that relates to your writing can be deducted as business expenses. According to the IRS, at the time of this writing, if your activity results in a profit any three of five consecutive years, you are presumed to be in business and your expenses are deductible. Therefore, it is important that you keep all receipts, no matter how small the amount, as they all add up at the end of the year.

Large items such as a computer, word processor, or typewriter can be depreciated over a period of years. See tax Schedule C for a sample form.

Legitimate expenses that are usually deductible, provided they relate to your writing as a *business,* include:

1. *Phone Calls*—I keep a running list on a separate pad near the phone and use a new page for each month noting the date, number, and to whom the call was made. When my phone bill arrives, I circle all business calls. If you have a separate business phone this of course will not be necessary; however, it is still advisable to keep track of all business calls for your own records.

2. *Classes*—College courses, such as regular college or university classes or workshops on *learning* to write (creative writing, language, and grammar) are usually not deductible. All career development and specialized or refresher classes (technical writing for publication, grammar for the business writer, and self-editing) are, however.

3. *Conferences* (business or career-related)—registration fees for conferences, seminars, workshops, and conventions; fees for having art or manuscripts critiqued

4. *Meals*—meals purchased while attending seminars, workshops, and conferences and lunch for people you are interviewing, using as a resource person, or who are helping you in some way with your writing

5. *Mileage*—and/or car expenses, air fares, parking, baggage handling, and tips

6. *Writing Supplies*—books, paper, pencils, magazines, dictionaries

7. *Office Supplies*—computer paper, printing ribbons, disks, envelopes, office machine repairs

8. *Dues*—for organizations, associations, clubs, and writing groups

9. *Postage*—stamps, Federal Express, or United Parcel Service fees

Many other miscellaneous items are also tax deductible—check the IRS publications.

Office in Your Home

Most authors work out of their homes, and a room in your home used exclusively for writing is generally accepted as a principal place of business.

Some accountants will tell you that if you have a small business operating out of your home, it often means a "red flag" to the IRS, and you are more apt to be selected for an audit. Even though the savings may not amount to a great deal, declaring your home as a place of business must be decided on an individual basis. If you keep good records, of course, you will have no problem proving you are in business; however, the time and inconvenience is bothersome and takes away from your writing time. Claiming your home as your place of business may also present some problems when you decide to sell your house. See IRS publication 523, "Selling Your Home."

When I first started writing, I checked with my accountant, and we decided that although I use one room in my home exclusively for writing and have a business license, the savings by declaring my home as my place of business would not justify the hassle and loss of my valuable time, not to mention his $200 an hour fee to represent me, if I should be called for audit. I suggest that upon receipt of your first check, you also talk with your accountant or tax preparer (whose fees are also tax deductible) or call the IRS's toll-free number, which can be found in the white pages of your telephone directory under U.S. Government—IRS.

Business License

Since writing is a business, some cities and counties require a business license. This is a simple matter (unless you have employees working for you), and the license can be applied for at your local city hall. The normal fee is approximately $25 per year. Having a license to operate a business can help establish your credibility as a business.

Your Profits

As your writing income increases, you may want to consider investing in a retirement plan. Programs such as IRAs allow you to invest up to $2,000 of your profits per year. U.S. Savings Bonds, annuities, and Keoghs are other plans you may want to check. See IRS publication 560, "Retirement Plans for the Self-Employed."

Some writers' organizations have health insurance plans for members, and if you do not have other health insurance, you may want to look into this. The Society of Children's Book Writers and Illustrators and the National Writer's Club are two organizations that offer such a plan. See the index for a list of writing organizations.

If you have been writing on a typewriter, you may want to consider purchasing a new computer or word processor or update your present system, all of which can be depreciated. A laser printer, new writing desk, or carpeting for your office (also deductible) might be other considerations.

18

The Art of Educational Promotion: How to Push Your Product

Promotion plans for your book, game, video, or other educational product will make a tremendous difference in how well it sells and how much money you make. Although book publishers have professional marketing staffs (experts in marketing), you should be willing to help promote your book or products in any way you can.

The first and most important way you can help with promotions is to carefully and thoroughly complete the "Author's Promotion Questionnaire," which most publishers send shortly after the return of your contract. Be sure to work up a comprehensive list of educators and organizations whom you would like the publisher to send review copies or sample products.

A well-thought-out plan on your part for self-promotion of your book, game, kit, or other product can have a positive effect toward wider recognition and higher sales. Start by making a list of anything you can do to further advance the sale of your product such as personal and professional contacts, your own speaking engagements, workshops where you are a presenter or participant, and media interviews. Your efforts will eventually pay off in increased sales, which result in an increase in royalties for you.

Discuss with your editor your ideas or plans for self-promoting your book or product. First ask how you can help, and then offer any suggestions you may have for promotions.

If you haven't done so already, this is the time to have business cards printed. Always carry a few with you, for you never know when the opportunity will arise to make a contact.

Ask your editor if the publicity or advertising department of your publishing firm can create a flyer giving an overview of your book or product along with ordering information. An 8½ × 11 flyer is the most convenient size for filing, carrying, and distributing. A picture of the front cover of your book and an overview of its contents, printed on colored paper, makes an attractive piece of advertising.

One of my editors had a master sheet made up for me that is updated when a new book comes out. I have five hundred or more copies printed (for quantity, printing is less expensive than photocopying) as I need them. I always carry a few copies with me, even when I go on vacations, for I can't resist visiting educational supply stores, children's bookstores, and sometimes the children's librarian when I visit another locality.

Joining professional writers' groups can help you make valuable contacts with other authors, publishers, editors, bookstores, and libraries, all of which can open new doors for you as an author and can also be of help with book promotions.

Being a part of an organization with which you have a common interest will help you get to know other authors and find out how they help promote their books, and will give you an opportunity to meet and get to know librarians and enlist their help in promoting your book by reading and sharing it with children, parents, and teachers.

Acknowledge or answer all letters you receive. When a teacher, parent, or librarian writes me about any of my books, I always reply and enclose flyers on my other books, mentioning to the writers that I feel they might be interested in knowing about other books I have written.

Reference book publishers such as Gale Research—publisher of

Something About the Author, edited by Anne Commire—may invite you to contribute a brief biography to their publication at no cost to you; however, some directories will list your biography only if you preorder a book.

Publicizing your book before publication can result in a mailing list for your publisher's advertising department. I gave a short overview of a forthcoming book of mine at a conference where I was presenting a workshop, and had a sign-up sheet available for those who wished to receive a notice on the publication of the book. This list was passed on to my editor. If your publisher is willing to provide them, prepublication flyers could also be distributed at meetings or workshops.

Personal Contacts

Personal contacts, although they require time and effort on your part, can often be one of your most effective advertising methods. If you live in or near a large metropolitan area, you may be able to personally contact a local book reviewer and lend a copy of your book for review, which could then lead to additional contacts. The more people you contact, the more people will pass on word of your book or product. It is amazing what word of mouth can do to increase sales.

Visiting schools, libraries, and bookstores armed with a few copies of your book(s), flyers, and a few publisher's catalogs (in a colorful tote bag or carrying case), can be a rewarding as well as a profitable experience. If possible, offer to spend a few hours autographing your book at bookstores and educational supply stores.

Ask yourself what types of businesses in addition to regular bookstores might buy your book. If it is geared to the needs of very young children (or new parents), try maternity shops, baby clothing and furniture stores or the baby department of a larger store—any of these might be interested in ordering copies.

Gift shops at museums carry books on science-related topics such as my books *Crystal Gardens* and *H_2O Science* and local history such as a book on the Alamo, or the Mississippi steam boats; arboretums stock books on botany and gardening such as my book

Gardening Fun; planetariums on space and astronomy—perhaps a puzzle book on the planets or a beginner's book on identifying the stars; and zoos handle books on almost any kind of animal—coloring, activity, or photo-essay books, plus the environment and ecology.

A nutrition education book that includes recipes might be purchased by kitchen or gourmet stores; a book on children's health, exercise, movement, or outdoor games might be handled by stores carrying sporting goods; and a craft store might be willing to display copies of your book of art activities for children.

If your product is a toy, game, or a learning kit, toy stores or party and gift shops might be interested in ordering.

A holiday book could be carried in almost any store or place of business around that particular holiday time.

It has been my experience that privately owned stores and shops are more willing to handle local authors' books or developers' products than are chain stores.

If you cannot make personal visits, you can make contacts by telephone; if time does not allow for either, then you may want to consider mailing flyers. I always attach my business card to flyers I mail and I add a brief note inviting them to call me if they have questions. Sending a flyer to parks and recreation leaders, Scouting programs, and boys' and girls' clubs might be appropriate for some books and products.

Speaking Engagements

The National Speakers Association (listed in the appendix) urges its members to "become an author" as one way to advance their speaking careers. Likewise for an author, becoming a good speaker may be a means of multiplying your book or product sales through speaking engagements, workshops, and teaching classes.

Some publishers put a notice of your availability as a speaker under your biographical sketch on the inside flap of the book jacket. I heard of one large publisher who, in later printings, listed the author's address under her name on the copyright page. Your editor may also make publishing sales reps aware that you are available as a speaker.

Check the Yellow Pages or the chamber of commerce for clubs and organizations in your city as well as surrounding towns, and make a list of potential groups that might be interested in hearing you speak on a topic on which you feel comfortable and qualified. Your talk should, of course, in some way relate to your product. Call or write explaining your subject, your availability, and if you expect a fee or honorarium. If appropriate, you may wish to ask for referrals and a letter of support when you give a presentation that is well received.

Libraries, colleges and universities, chambers of commerce, and convention bureaus usually have speakers' lists available. If this appeals to you, call and find out about adding your name to the list.

Since local writers' clubs will be interested in writing for the educational market, you might consider volunteering to speak or serve on a panel at a local meeting, workshop, or conference. Most groups pay a small honorarium and offer to sell your books.

Other groups I have found to be interested in educational authors and have invited me to speak are Pen Women, Head Start, child day care providers, and Friends of the Library (for addresses, see the appendix).

Offer to read your book, do a craft, teach songs, or read your poetry at a bookstore (maybe a children's story hour) that sells the type of books you write. Not only will they order copies of your book but they will also no doubt hold an autographing party. For added publicity, ask the store manager if you can notify the newspaper of your event. They may print a notice of the event as well as do a follow-up article on you or on your presentation.

Conferences and Conventions—Speaking at educationally related conferences is a way of reaching a large group of people who would be potential purchasers of your product. I have presented workshops at local, state, and national conferences. At some as few as 15 people attended my session; at others 500 to 800 attended. In some cases no honorarium was given; however, the conference registration was paid as well as most of my meals. Other times I have received all expenses, or one or more of the following: travel, meals, registration, hotel accommodations, and an honorarium.

Honoraria—For speakers presenting a one-hour session, an honorarium may average from $50 to $150 for a small conference and for a large conference from $200 to $400. Well-known and keynote speakers receive from $500 to $5,000. Often the conference committee has a set speaker's fee; other times a presenter may be asked the amount he or she charges. After you become known, you may be able to set your own fee schedule, but even in the beginning if you decide to accept speaking engagements you should be prepared to quote your fee and whether you expect travel expenses, meals, or other amenities. Occasionally I speak without an honorarium, but only if I especially want to attend the conference and feel it will help promote my products. However, I feel strongly that if an organization is charging more than a modest registration fee, it should be able to compensate good speakers—for the speakers make the conference.

If you are going to be presenting at a large or a national conference (see the appendix for a listing), be sure to notify your editor, because your editor or someone from the publishing house may be attending and may also have a display booth. You may be invited (you can always volunteer) to spend a couple hours in the booth autographing your books for customers. However, having the opportunity to meet your editor and discuss some of your new ideas—possibly at lunch—is a valuable experience in itself.

At one California state conference where I was speaking (and autographing my books), the president of one of the major educational companies I was writing for hosted a party for his four local authors and his clients from a three-state area. We authors felt like celebrities! A similar event occurred over a period of several years with an educational magazine publisher for whom I was writing. The editor-in-chief hosted a party for local authors and clients at one of the top Beverly Hills hotels. Not only did I meet several staff members from the magazine and their clients but I also had a chance to get to know some of their other authors and exchange experiences with them.

When I attend conferences, conventions, and workshops, I take along extra flyers to place on the "freebie table." If I know one of our local educational supply or bookstores will be exhibiting at a nearby conference where I am speaking, I contact the owners three months in advance to let them know, and I also mention the books

I will be discussing in my talk. This way, they can order copies for participants to purchase. Then during my workshop, I inform the audience that my books are available at Brown's Teacher's Store, booth number twenty-three, and the hours I will be there to autograph my books.

In lieu of payment or an honorarium, you may want to use the barter system as I have. Several times a year, I speak at health spas in exchange for one to three days as a guest. I do short talks on keeping a journal, writing memoirs, and getting published. With each talk, I am able to share a few of my books, and consequently have met teachers, media aides, and librarians who were interested in ordering my books. Naturally, I handed each a flyer with my business card attached. Book sales and invitations to speak may result from this gesture (I had a free, enjoyable minivacation).

If speaking in public is a new experience for you and you are uncomfortable speaking to groups of people, you may find joining Toastmasters/Toastmistress to be helpful. You can usually find announcements of their meetings listed in your local newspaper or you can obtain information from the chamber of commerce (see the appendix for the national address).

You may also find it helpful to make an outline of your talk, tape or make a video, and then play it back. This can give you an idea of how you sound, the length of your talk, and how you may want to improve it.

School and Library Visits

Schools and libraries usually welcome authors and/or illustrators who are willing to share their book with students or library patrons.

Schools—Many schools today have annual book fairs or author days where several authors and/or illustrators visit a class and talk about their work. Once you speak at one of these events, your name usually gets placed on a circulating school author's master list and you may get more calls than you can work into your time schedule and find you have to limit the number you accept.

The sponsoring organization, PTA, or other parent group, often holds an autograph party at the school or a central library where parents, teachers, librarians, and students come to buy the author's books and have them autographed. Although these events are fulfilling experiences, it can be a long, tiring day. You have to decide if the effort and time involved offset the opportunity to promote your book.

When speaking at schools, I arrive early and set up my books along with flyers in the teachers' lunch room. Sometimes I present a review of my books to the teachers while they are having lunch. Whenever I speak at a school, I always donate a copy of one of my books, along with few flyers on my other books, to the school library. Never miss an opportunity to promote your book!

Your time is valuable and speaking takes you away from your writing, so authors should not be expected to speak for free. I do free author visits only at schools my grandchildren attend or where my sons teach. The standard honorarium in California for authors at school authors' fairs is $100 to $150 for two to five sessions, plus lunch and sometimes breakfast. Well-known authors who speak at schools on their own charge $200 to $300 per day with award-winning authors receiving $500 to over $1,000 per day plus expenses.

Don't overlook parochial and private schools as a source for author visits (see listing in the appendix). Most have parent groups that may be willing to provide your honorarium.

Our local reading association holds a county-wide book fair where they display books students have written. Parents, teachers, principals, librarians, and siblings also attend, and local authors and illustrators are invited. We are provided with a table for displaying our books where we talk with students and sign autographs. Lunch is provided and a local bookstore orders and sells our books. On my table, I may display finger puppets, cut-out stories, and a crystal salt garden—all examples from my books— to attract visitors, and as always I pass out flyers. An illustrator may display sketches or the dummy of a picture book; a photographer may exhibit photographs and camera equipment used for a photo-essay book.

Preschool and Child Care Programs—If you write for very young children, speaking to preschoolers might also be a possibility.

Since many are either church or privately operated, they may be able to offer only a small honorarium or none at all (see the appendix for national listings).

A local child care center director who had purchased my hat book, invited me to lead their hat parade. They had invited a newspaper feature writer, who brought along a photographer. Although I expected no honorarium, I felt this was good publicity for a half hour of my time; the next day an article including a listing of several of my books and the local store where they could be purchased, appeared in the paper.

Head Start, state preschool programs, and college and university lab schools usually give honoraria or pay a fee for visiting authors. Talk with any or all of these groups about the possibility of doing an author or in-service visit based on your writing interests.

Generally one is compensated for doing in-service training, and I have found this to be true for Head Start, church-related, private, and adult education preschool programs.

I have also been invited to present short evening workshops at educational supply stores and allowed to choose my own topic. The owner gives me a small honorarium, orders extra copies of my books to sell, serves refreshments, and allows time for browsing the bookstore and making purchases.

If the schools in your area do not have author visitation programs, contact your local school parent group or reading association and suggest the idea, offering to be their first visiting author. Explain that you will read portions of your book and share information on writing a book and getting it published. It is good business practice to put your invitation in writing, stating the days and hours you are available and the honorarium you expect. Some schools follow up a visit with an autograph party for the author and offer the author's books for sale.

Libraries — You can promote your book by volunteering to read your book at story hour, or a book for older children at a Saturday or summer library program. Offer to do a book talk for a children's librarian staff meeting or the Friends of the Library group in your area.

In the past I have volunteered to do a series of parent workshops in two different cities for parents of preschoolers attending library story hours. Each five-week session is based on or includes material from my books; the theme is "for you and your child." Examples are on making your own modeling doughs (from my book *Magic Mixtures*), crafts (*Hats, Hats, and More Hats*), kitchen gardening (*Gardening Fun*), exercises (*Holiday Movement Activities*), and puppets and language (*Fingerlings: Finger Puppets*).

Even if your book is a paperback, libraries often purchase copies and then have them rebound with reinforced binding for library use.

Article Writing

Writing articles for educational and parenting magazines and newsletters, with a sentence or two mentioning the book you have authored, is another way to help promote your book, plus you will also receive payment from the publisher for your article.

See chapters 13, 14, and 15 on writing and submitting to different types of magazines and newsletters.

Radio and Television Promotion and Publicity

Contact local radio and television stations to see if they interview authors. Call and talk with them, or send a letter of introduction, a short bio, and any clips or tear sheets on your book or product. State your interest in being interviewed, including any humorous events you can recall (the emcee and the audience like humor), and then ask if you can send a copy of your book. If you are interviewed, they will probably return your copy of the book.

I suggest you do not send a copy of your book without calling first. The general manager of a medium-size radio station told me they receive over a hundred books a year from authors who want to be interviewed on their station and that most are never read. Your best chance for a radio interview might be with your local or hometown radio station, especially if you know someone who works there.

Radio interviews may be done live at the station or over the telephone. For telephone interviews, you will be told the time you will be called. If you're not told, find out what type of questions you will be asked and make a note of how you will answer. It has been my experience that you don't need to worry too much about what you will say, because the interviewer does most of the talking.

Television stations are not too willing to interview authors unless they have won a big award or are well known, and invitations are seldom given to children's book authors or educational book authors. However, they may be interested from an educational view, such as relating an interview to reading, math, or science. Public television stations seem to be more conducive to authors writing for children or on education. You might contact them about having you read from your book, share an activity, or demonstrate your game or other product, especially on a program geared to the audience of your book.

Radio/TV Interview Reports (215-259-1070), Lansdowne, Pennsylvania, producers of a newsletter for radio and television, sell ads in their newsletter for authors who have a strong desire to be interviewed. However, the cost is approximately $300.

Teaching Classes and Seminars

If you are teaching, ask your principal if you can share your book or product at a teacher's meeting or present a miniworkshop on how to use it in the classroom.

Teaching for a college or university usually requires a master's degree, and adult education instructors generally need an adult education credential. However, noncredit classes and community education classes do not.

The following is a list of sources to investigate if you want to consider teaching a class in relation to your book or product. And, as mentioned previously, teaching a course can lead to writing another book and can give you ideas for magazine articles.

• Colleges and universities—short courses, extension classes, Saturday seminars, noncredit classes on educational topics.

• Adult education programs offered through high schools or

community colleges—refresher classes on English, math, or history, making reference to your book or using your worksheets.

• In-service teacher training classes offered through your local or county school district—attendees can make environmental crafts based on ideas using your Earth Day craft book; write their own computer software program based on your how-to book on classroom computer programs; or discover new directions in geography for the elementary grades using examples from your geography workbook.

• Community center programs—adult programs dealing with how to write, how to create a new game, how you can help your grandchildren learn to read, how to have fun with maps, or how to discover the world, based on your book, worksheets, or game.

• Classes through parks and recreation departments—Read through the catalogs to see what is being offered and decide if your book or product might work into a class for adults or kids.

• Classes for older citizens offered through recreation programs, community centers, or senior programs—help participants plan a trip (referring to maps, customs, and historical sites) using your geography or history workbook (or supplemental textbook); compile their own family recipe book using your cookbook as a guide for getting started, classifying recipes, and adding photographs; or write their memoirs or keep a journal.

• Summer classes for children offered through summer school programs, the YMCA, or Boys' and Girls' Clubs—teach kids exercise and creative movement based on your exercise book; or teach youngsters to eat healthy using your book on nutrition as a guide.

I teach Saturday classes on writing and on special early childhood classes (all relating to my books) at several universities and colleges in three different states. Three of these are located in cities where family members live (which provides me a place to stay) and the others are places where I like to vacation.

If you are interested in teaching a class as a means of promoting your book or product, write up a description of the class and send your résumé or bio along with a letter of introduction to the director of the program. For names and addresses of institutions and organizations, start with your local telephone directory.

Three months prior to the date of my scheduled classes, I send a note about my class and flyers on my books to bookstores and teacher supply stores in the city where the class will be held as well as those in surrounding towns. They usually respond telling me which books they do or will stock.

You may find *An Author's Guide to Children's Book Promotions* by Susan Salzman Raab helpful on planning your self-promoting strategy. Although it does not cover educational materials specifically, the author offers suggestions on helping your publisher, and on school, library, and bookstore promotions. For ordering information, write to Raab Associates, 19 Price Lane, Rose Valley, PA 19065.

Selling Your Products

Some publishers offer their authors the opportunity to buy copies of their books for resale. The discount is usually 40 percent, the same as to retailers, and some even pay shipping charges. Other companies frown on this policy, as it means authors are competing against stores where they regularly sell through their sales reps.

Since we do not have a teacher supply store in my city, I order books from one of my publishers, who encourages authors to buy books for resale, to sell at some workshops I present. Payment is due on delivery, and I also pay shipping costs and California state sales tax. That way I can resell the books without bothering to collect sales tax; however, I must file and pay sales tax, if due, at the beginning of each year.

If your state has a sales tax, you will need to apply to your State Board of Equalization for a resale tax number. The service is free and requires filing (on forms provided to you) and paying sales tax the first of each year. You may also need a business license (see chapter 17).

If your product is a game, jigsaw puzzle, or learning kit, you may want to consider promoting it through a "party plan." Many products are sold successfully in this way. This will take extra time and planning, and before you start it would be a good idea to talk with someone who sells through a party plan such as those selling jewelry, cosmetics, toys, household items, and clothing. These sources can be found in the Yellow Pages.

You may also want to write to the Public Relations Society of America, 33 Irving Place, 3rd floor, New York, NY 10003-2376.

19

A Time to Write: The Success Connection

WHAT DO YOU MEAN, YOU DON'T HAVE TIME TO write? When is the right time to write? By the time you have reached this chapter, you may have already started writing. If you haven't, start now! James Russell Lowell said, "If one waits for the right time to come before writing, the right time never comes." Now is the right time to write!

Time—how do you use it? Maybe you need to rearrange your priorities, organize your life, decide what has to be done today, tomorrow, and next week so you will have time to write.

What's the difference between someone who writes and a real writer? Answer: a published writer. Published writers write.

Accept the fact that you are probably never going to have the leisure time to sit down and write a book from beginning to end. You can't give up everything—don't neglect your family or yourself, but sometimes it is necessary to ignore the laundry, let the house go, forget about grocery shopping or even preparing meals—and just write. If not a book, maybe a short story, poem, or an article for a magazine, a game, or a puzzle. To be productive, writing has to be something we want to do and that we enjoy, and we have to make writing a part of our daily lives. If you consider writing a luxury, something you do (if there is time) only after you have taken care of the countless other duties and chores you think you have to do, then you are not writing for publication, you are writing as a hobby. If your goal is to get published, writing is more than a hobby. It becomes your second vocation and requires appropriate time and attention.

Managing Time

You have decided to write but . . . "I can't *find* time to write"; "I must *make* time to write"; "There never seems to be *enough* time to write." These are statements I have heard from students in my writing classes. If you want to write, don't be guilty of using any of these excuses, and that's what they are, excuses—for not writing.

You don't *make* time; there are only twenty-four hours in a day. Start by using thirty minutes of each day to write. Then increase the time gradually. Soon you will be writing for hours.

You don't *find* time and you don't *lose* time. If you can't write every day at the beginning, try setting aside a half day two or three times a week for writing.

There is *enough* time to write if you really want to be a writer. If you can't write every day or two or three times a week, setting aside one day a week for writing might work best for you. Although I write nearly every day, Wednesday is my full day for writing. I try not to make any appointments or commitments and no shopping, baking, or extra household tasks on Wednesdays—just writing.

It all adds up to how badly you want to write, not how busy you are. Here are some specific ways you can save time and use time for writing:

• Decide when during the twenty-four-hour period of each day is the best time for you to write—early morning, after lunch or dinner, while the kids are in school, after the kids go to bed.

• Occasionally be a night owl: As an experiment for one week, stay up an hour later each night to write. After one week, compare what you've written with daytime efforts. I do some of my best work between 10:00 and 12:00 P.M., but not every night. Try the same experiment for five early mornings in a row. Maybe you work better on the dawn patrol.

• Try making a list to see how you spend your time. Write down how you spend each twenty-four-hour period every day for a week. Take a good look at your average day. A good place to start might be the number of hours of television you watch and how much time you spend talking on the telephone. A study on time management showed these to be the two biggest time robbers. Study your list and you will be surprised to find how many hours you can't account for or how many are wasted every day. Total your wasted time—this is the time you could be using for writing.

Setting Goals

I don't make New Year's resolutions, and I don't know anyone who makes them and keeps them. However, I do set goals for myself, both long-range and short-term, and I do meet most of them. As a matter of fact, I make several sets of goals—goals for self; for home and family; for writing; for church and community projects; and for travel and trips.

It is okay to dream big, but set realistic goals for yourself and work toward them. What is realistic? In my case, after I had 4 or 5 magazine items published, I set myself a goal for 25, then 50, 100, and now my long-range goal is for 500. When my first book was published, I set a goal for 10, then 20, and now my goal is 50! I set a goal for a religious book and 2 were published; for a supplemental, nonfiction book (2 published); for a picture book (although I have 3 picture book manuscripts off to publishers, I have not sold any, but I will).

Believe in yourself—believe you are a writer! It is okay for authors to have a strong writing ego!

Along with goals you need to set priorities. Which of your goals is the most important? Put them at the top of your list, or circle the important ones in red, as I do, and then number them in order of their importance to you.

Writer's Block

What is writer's block? Since I have never experienced it, I tend to feel it may be just another excuse for not writing. No doubt you will find yourself stuck at times, but if you can't get the introduction or the first paragraph or chapter started, skip it and go on to the next part. Write what you can and then go back and fill in.

Don't sit thinking and waiting for inspiration—write! Begin where you have something to say. On the other hand, don't waste your time just writing anything, but put down specific words that relate to your project. One word or a sentence may be just the right inspiration you need. Try this: Make a simple random list of topics. Put them in alphabetical order, just as an exercise. Then choose the first word or last item in the list, and write about it for five minutes. Then stop! A nonsense exercise like this can get words flowing. Here's another idea: If your interest is science, start writing about your favorite animal or insect; if it's history, write about a historical period during which you would like to have lived; if it is geography, write about a place or country you would like to visit. Each of these exercises could develop into books, magazine articles, stories, puzzles, or quizzes.

Interesting exercises for dealing with writer's block appear in *The Practice of Poetry: Writing Exercises from Poets Who Teach* edited by Robin Behn and Chase Twichell (HarperCollins, paperback). You don't have to be a poet to benefit from these helpful ideas from master teachers of writing.

Take a Break

Regardless of whatever time you have set aside for writing, you will want to take short breaks now and then. Muscle tension builds up quickly during long writing periods. Stop for a few minutes and make a cup of tea, go the kitchen for a glass of water or a snack, or walk at a good pace from room to room a few times. If I am at my desk for long intervals, I find that a walk around the backyard revitalizes me. I may stop to smell the flowers or cut a few to bring into my office. But a word of caution, don't let garden or household tasks distract from your writing. A few slow stretching exercises and several deep breaths—good tension-releasers—can also provide a relaxing break while seated at your desk.

By the way, on these short breaks, I always leave my word processor *on* so I can get right back to my work and won't be tempted to do something else.

Ah, the Sweet Smell of Success

No matter how many books an author has had published, every one of us started as an unpublished writer. And, yes, you will receive rejection slips—everyone does.

Isabel Wilner, a teacher, wrote *A Christmas Alphabet*, which started its journey toward publication in 1958. However, it wasn't until thirty-three years later that it was finally accepted for publication by Dutton Children's Books with a new name, *B Is for Bethlehem*. The first printing was 20,000 copies!

In a recent writer's association newsletter, I read about Marcia Bylalick, who, after twenty-four rejections, sold her first book to an imprint of Harcourt Brace Jovanovich. *It's a Matter of Trust* is due out in the fall of 1994.

Miracles seem to happen to those who write educational material.

Reneé Harmon's first book, *The Actor's Survival in Today's Film Industry,* was inspired by acting classes she taught at a California college. Five more books have followed.

Leonard Mogel left full-time magazine publishing and wrote his first book on the media profession, now in its third edition, with over 80,000 copies in print. A series of three books developed out of continuing education classes he was teaching—*Making It in Public Relations, Making It in Broadcasting,* and *Making It in Books and Magazines.* A fourth book will soon be added to the series.

As a teacher at the Massachusetts Audubon Society for many years, Edith Sisson had been keeping a file on her classes. An editor who saw her classes listed in a newsletter, asked her if she would consider writing a book based on her classes. With the encouragement from the editor, she decided to put the ideas and activities she had developed into a book. *Nature for Children of All*

Ages, her first book, has over 100,000 copies in print. Her second book, *Animals in the Family,* which contains photographs (some of which she took), received several rejections and was even turned down by an agent before it was published.

Administration of Schools for Young Children (now in its fourth edition, Delmar Publishers) by Phyllis Click developed out of classes she taught for teachers at local colleges. A soon-to-be published book is on school-age child care. Phyllis also cowrote with her husband student study guides on human development for the junior college level. How did this happen? Her husband brought home a flyer announcing that a publisher was looking for qualified people to write study guides. On the basis of an outline, sample chapter, and résumé, they received a contract. From then on, they continued to receive additional assignments.

A first book on physics for elementary-age children was Janice VanCleave's (a classroom teacher for twenty-six years) first book. The book, published in 1985, is still in print. It was difficult getting her second book (*Chemistry for Every Kid*) accepted by a publisher, but with persistence and determination her second effort found a home with John Wiley Publishers, and she went on to write twenty books for them. Her best-selling books *Biology for Every Kid, Math for Every Kid,* and *Earth Science for Every Kid* continue to receive glowing reviews, and she even has a fan club with thousands of members! Since most of her books are science related (though she has books on geography, math, and geometry to be published soon), she now takes her "science show" on the road, visiting young scientists in museums, bookstores, libraries, and schools. Her publisher flew her to New York to meet the staff and then sent her on a publicity tour into schools across the country.

For many years, Carolyn Luetje taught preschool at her church. Her writing experience included Bible school and Sunday school curriculums, which she wrote for her denominational publisher. Her first book, *Action Rhymes,* was the result of meeting the editor of a small educational publishing house at a reception sponsored by an educational magazine editor with whom she had worked. She and a friend have since coauthored eight teacher resource books.

Then there is Linda Turrell, a library skills teacher and school librarian, and her miracle. She had an idea for a series of books on library skills and organization information for research projects for children in kindergarten through eighth grade. "I thought, Why don't I sit down over the summer and write the books," she said. However, it took her two years to write the books and two and a half years to find a publisher.

Along the way, her manuscript got rerouted, sent from one editor to another, ended up in a special-project department, and eventually got lost. After all of this, she then sent for publishers' catalogs, studied them and the *Children's Writer's & Illustrator's Market,* made a new photocopy of her manuscript, and sent it off to another publisher. Linda says she "came close to placing the series with the publisher," but was asked to resubmit it next year because of budget restrictions. Discouraged? Yes. But Linda didn't give up. She discovered T.S. Denison, a supplementary educational publisher, and again the manuscript was sent off. Ten days later, much to her surprise and overwhelming joy, she received not one, but *five* contracts, one for another book the publisher was asking her to write. "Imagine that," she said, "I just had something at the right time that they needed!" And that's not all, Linda has a contract from another editor for another book and is working on several more.

For those who view landing that first contract as an impossible dream, Linda says, "Never give up! I like to think of those trite but true words: You knock on door after door and hear no, but it only takes one door to open to hear the first yes."

These authors all received rejection slips, but none of them gave up—they are examples of *real* writers! It took a while in some cases, but they all did get their first book published.

You Can Do It, Too!

Are you a procrastinator? Do you say to yourself any of the following? "I'll start writing after I grade these papers . . . after I retire . . . when the kids get into school . . . after the kids graduate . . . during my vacation . . . during spring break . . . in the summer when there is less going on . . . during the winter on those long dark, cold nights . . . tomorrow or next week for sure—I'll have more time then." But, you won't. Now is the time!

Remember, you can't be a writer if you don't write, you can't write if you don't put something on paper, and you won't get published if you don't finish your project and get it in the mail.

Don't give up on yourself, your manuscript, or your idea. If it is good keep sending it out, for if it is good, a publisher will buy it; if it isn't good enough, rewrite it and send it to another publisher.

You have twenty-four hours each day, just like the rest of us. Use your time wisely and you will have time to write, and with persistence you, too, *will* get published—I know you will, because it happened to me!

APPENDIX

OPPORTUNITIES FOR TEACHER/WRITERS

Across the curriculum approach
Action rhymes
Activity books
Activity cards
After school programs
Aides in the classroom
Alphabet activities
Art projects
Atlases
Audio cassettes
Audiovisuals
Awards
Basal programs
Bilingual education
Blackboard games
Board games
Books
Book markers
Book reports

Bulletin board ideas
Calendars
Celebrations
Certificates
Charts
Circle time
Classroom management
Coteaching
Cognitive development
Colors
Computer books
Computer education games
Computer software
Concepts
Consonants
Cooking experiences
Crafts
Creative movement
Creative thinking tasks

Critical thinking skills
Cross-cultural experiences
Cultures
Dictionaries
Discovery centers
Discrimination tasks
Drama
Dramatic play
Duplicating masters
Electronic games
Encyclopedias
English language
Enrichment programs
ESL programs
Ethnic studies
Exercises
Filmstrips
Fingerplays
Flannelgraphs
Flash cards
Foreign languages
Games
Gardening
Geography
Gifted students
Guides for the curriculum
Handicapped programs
Health
Hearing impaired
History
Holidays
Homework tips
Importance of play
Individualized learning
Integrated learning
Instructional aids
Lab activities
Language arts

Learning centers
Learning toys and games
Lesson plans
Literature
Literature-based programs
Kits for teachers and students
Magazines in the classroom
Magnetic board materials
Manipulatives
Maps
Matching cards and games
Mathematics
Media
Mentor teachers
Minilessons
Motion pictures
Movement and motor
    development activities
Music
Nutrition
Numbers
Opposites
Overhead transparencies
Papercraft
Parent education
Parent communication
Pattern books
Parts of speech
Penmanship
Photo-essay books
Photography
Physical education
Picture cards
Plays
Poetry
Posters
Preschool programs
Problem solving

Puppetry
Puzzles
Quizzes
Reading
Reading comprehension
Reference books
Reproducibles
Resource books
Rewards
Riddle books
Science
Scripts
Sensory experiences
Shapes
Social studies
Songs
Sorting experiences
Spelling
Special education
Stamp making and printing
Stickers
Story starters
Storytelling
Storytelling aids and props
Study prints
Substitute teaching

Supplementary books and
   materials
Table games
Tactile experiences
Task cards
Teaching tools
Teacher assistants
Teacher resource books and aids
Teacher tips
Telling time
Testing
Textbooks
Thematic units
Theme books
Toddler programs
Videos
Visual aids
Vocabulary skills
Volunteers in the classroom
Vowels
Whole language
Word building
Workbooks
Worksheets
Writing
Year-round school

TRENDS IN PUBLISHING

Books come in multiple formats:

hardcover and paperback

three-ring binder and plastic comb binders

flash cards or picture cards

interactive formats: consumable units/workbooks, worksheets

nontraditional sizes—foldouts, 3-D, Big Books, paper sculpture, pop-up, pull tab, lift the flap

audio tapes

videos

filmstrips and film

videodiscs

computer diskettes

electronic access (like CompuServe)

spin-off products such as calendars, daybooks, diaries, postcards, notepaper—all tied in with books

special editions for special markets: large print, braille, limited vocabulary, condensed, teaching/annotated editions

support materials

learning tapes

subscription formats—newsletters, magazines, and books in serial form

EDUCATIONAL MARKET DIRECTORY

Publishers of Student,
Teacher, and Classroom Aids

Acropolis Books, Ltd.
13950 Park Center Road
Herndon, VA 22071

Addison-Wesley Publishing
    Company
2725 Sand Hill Road
Menlo Park, CA 94025

Alleyside Press
Box 889
Hagerstown, MD 21741

American Teaching Aids
6442 City West Parkway,
    Ste. 300
Eden Prairie, MN 55344

BGR Publishing
4520 N. 12th Street
Phoenix, AZ 85014

Belair Publications, USA
P.O. Box 61612
Venice, FL 34292

Charlesbridge Publishing
85 Main Street
Watertown, MA 02172

Continental Press
Elizabethtown, PA 17022-
    2299

Creative Teaching Press
P.O. Box 6017
Cypress, CA 90630-0017

Creatively Yours Puppetry
P.O. Box 226
Ankeny, IA 50021

Curriculum Associates, Inc.
5 Esquire Road
North Billerica, MA 01862-
1589

Delta Education, Inc.
P.O. Box 950
Hudson, NH 03051

Demco's Kids & Things
Box 7488
Madison, WI 53707

T.S. Denison & Company, Inc.
9601 Newton Avenue South
Minneapolis, MN 55431-2509

Didax Educational Resources
395 Main Street
Rowley, MA 01969

Delmar Publishers, Inc.
2 Computer Drive
Albany, NY 12212

Easy Aids, Inc.
9402½ Compton Boulevard
Bellflower, CA 90706-3009

Education Center Inc.
1607 Battleground Avenue
P.O. Box 9753
Greensboro, NC 27429

Educational Development Corporation
103302 E. 55th Place
Tulsa, OK 74146

Educational Insights
19560 S. Rancho Way
Dominguez Hills, CA 90220

ESP Publishers, Inc.
7163 123rd Circle North
Largo, FL 34643

Evan-Moor Corporation
18 Lower Ragsdale Drive
Monterey, CA 93940

Eye Gate Media
3333 Elston Avenue
Chicago, IL 60618

Fearon Teacher Aids
442 City West Parkway, Ste.
300
Eden Prairie, MN 55344

Front Row Experience
540 Discovery Bay Boulevard
Byron, CA 94514

Good Apple
6442 City West Parkway, Ste.
300
Eden Prairie, MN 55344

Gryphon House
Early Childhood Books
P.O. Box 275
Mt. Rainier, MD 20712

Hands On Teaching Materials,
    Inc.
P.O. Box 11397
Raleigh, NC 27604

Hayes School Publishing Co.,
    Inc.
321 Pennwood Avenue
Wilkinsburg, PA 15221

D.C. Heath and Company
125 Spring Street
Lexington, MA 02173

High Reach Learning, Inc.
36 Old Shoals Road
Arden, NC 28704

Humanics Publishing Group
1482 Mecaslin Street
Atlanta, GA 30309

Incentive Publications, Inc.
3835 Cleghorn Avenue
Nashville, TN 37215

Instructor Books
730 Broadway
New York, NY 10003

Judy/Instructo
6442 City West Parkway, Ste.
    300
Eden Prairie, MN 55344

Just Us Books
301 Main Street, Ste. 22–24
Orange, NJ 07050

Leadership Publishers, Inc.
P.O. Box 8358
Des Moines, IA 50301-8358

Learned and Tested
1627 Woodland Avenue
Austin, TX 78741

The Learning Works
P.O. Box 6187, Dept. G
Santa Barbara, CA 93106

Milliken Publishing Company
P.O. Box 21579
St. Louis, MO 63162-0579

Modern Curriculum Press
13900 Prospect Road
Cleveland, OH 44136

Open Court Publishing Co.
315 Fifth Street
Peru, IL 61354

Phoenix Learning Resources
2345 Chaffee Road
St. Louis, MO 63146

Pleasant Company
P.O. Box 998
Middleton, WI 53562-0998

Price/Stern/Sloan
360 N. La Cienega Boulevard
Los Angeles, CA 90048

R & E Publishers
P.O. Box 2008
Saratoga, CA 95070

Redleaf Press
450 N. Syndicate, Ste. 5
St. Paul, MN 55104-4125

Rhythm Productions
Box 34485
Los Angeles, CA 90034

Saddleback Educational, Inc.
711 W. 17th Street, Ste. F-12
Costa Mesa, CA 92627

Frank Schaffer Publications,
   Inc.
23740 Hawthorne Boulevard
P.O. Box 2853, Dept. 443
Torrance, CA 90509-2853

Scholastic Professional Books
730 Broadway
New York, NY 10003

Dale Seymour Publications
P.O. Box 10888
Palo Alto, CA 94303-0879

Tom Snyder Productions, Inc.
80 Coolidge Hill Road
Watertown, MA 02172

Sterling Publishing Co.
387 Park Avenue South
New York, NY 10016

Tab Books
Division of McGraw-Hill, Inc.
Blue Ridge Summit, PA 17294-
   0850

Teacher College Press
1234 Amsterdam Avenue
New York, NY 10027

Teacher Created Material, Inc.
P.O. Box 1878
Huntington Beach, CA 92647

Teacher's Little Pal Company
Box 251
Rawlings, MD 21557

Toys To Grow On
P.O. Box 17
Long Beach, CA 90801

Trend Enterprises, Inc.
P.O. Box 19069
Denver, CO 80219

Troll Associates, Inc.
Watermill Press
100 Corporate Drive
Mahwah, NJ 07430

Troubador Press
11150 Olympic Boulevard
Los Angeles, CA 90064

J. Weston Walch, Publisher
321 Valley Street
P.O. Box 658
Portland, ME 04104-0658

The Wright Group
19201 120th Avenue NE
Bothell, WA 98011-9512

Wieser Educational, Inc.
30085 Comercio, Dept. E93
Rancho Santa Margarita, CA
   92688

Workman Publishing Co.
708 Broadway
New York, NY 10003

WonderStorm
Sundance Publisher
1278 West Ninth Street
Cleveland, OH 44113-1067

CURRICULUM-ORIENTED
BOOK PUBLISHERS

Barron's Educational Series,
 Inc.
250 Wireless Boulevard
Hauppauge, NY 11788

Childrens Press, Inc.
5440 N. Cumberland Avenue
Chicago, IL 60656

Creative Education
P.O. Box 277
Mankato, MN 56001

Dillon Press
866 Third Avenue
New York, NY 10022

Facts On File
460 Park Avenue South
New York, NY 10016

D.C. Heath and Company
125 Spring Street
Lexington, MA 02173

Houghton Mifflin
Educational Books
2 Park Street
Boston, MA 02108

Kane Publishing Services, Inc.
222 East 46th Street
New York, NY 10017

Kingfisher Books
95 Madison Avenue
New York, NY 10016

Lerner Publications, Inc.
241 First Avenue North
Minneapolis, MN 55401

Julian Messner
Silver Burdett Press
15 Columbus Circle
New York, NY 10023

Millbrook Press, Inc.
2 Old New Milford Road
Box 335
Brookfield, CT 06804

Parenting Press, Inc.
P.O. Box 75267
Seattle, WA 98125

Raintree/Steck-Vaughn Pub-
    lishers
11 Prospect Street
Madison, NJ 07940

Silver Press
250 James Street
Morrison, NJ 07960

Twenty-First Century
115 W. 18th Street
New York, NY 10011

Franklin Watts
5450 North Cumberland Ave-
    nue
Chicago, IL 60656

TEXTBOOK PUBLISHERS

Fearon/Janus/Quercus
Simon & Schuster Educational
　Group
500 Harbor Boulevard
Belmont, CA 94002

Glencoe
Macmillan/McGraw-Hill
15319 Chatsworth Street
Mission Hills, CA 91346-9609

Harcourt Brace, School Pub-
　lishers
6277 Sea Harbor Drive
Orlando, FL 32887

Holt, Rinehart & Winston,
　Inc.
School Division Headquarters
1627 Woodland Avenue
Austin, TX 78741

Kendall/Hunt Publishing Com-
　pany
2460 Kerper Boulevard
Dubuque, IA 52001

Barnell Loft, Ltd.
958 Church Street
Baldwin, NY 11510

Macmillan/McGraw-Hill
School Divison
220 East Danieldale Road
De Soto, TX 75115

Merrill Publishing Company
1300 Alum Creek Drive
P.O. Box 508
Columbus, OH 43216

Random House Publishers
School Division
201 E. 50th Street
New York, NY 10022

ScottForesman
Division of HarperCollins Publishers
1900 East Lake Avenue
Glenview, IL 60025

Silver Burdett Ginn
P.O. Box 2649
Columbus, OH 43216-2649

Sundance Publishers
P.O. Box 1826
Littleton, MA 01460

Zaner-Bloser, Inc.
P.O. Box 16764
Columbus, OH 43216-6764

NONBOOK MARKETS

Alpha Books
11711 N. College Avenue
Carmel, IN 46023
(computer books—authors,
    illustrators)

American Arts and Graphics
10915 47th Avenue West
Mukileto, WA 98275
(posters)

Ampersand Press
691 26th Street
Oakland, CA 94612
(science games)

AV Concept Corporation
30 Montauk Boulevard
Oakdale, NY 11769
(scripts, filmstrips, computer
    program software)

Clearvue/eav
6465 N. Avondale
Chicago, IL 60631
(videotapes, slide sets, film-
    strips)

Educational Images, Ltd.
P.O. Box 3456
Elmira, NY 14907
(multimedia kits, slide sets)

Educational Insights
Dept. WM
1905 S. Rancho Way
Dominguez Hills, CA 90220
(charts, study prints, tapes, cas-
    settes)

Educational Video Network
1401 19th Street
Huntsville, TX 77340
(videotapes, scripts, video
    graphics)

Gateway Productions, Inc.
3011 Magazine Street
New Orleans, LA 70115
(social studies filmstrips)

Highlights for Children
803 Church Street
Honesdale, PA 18431
(activity books)

Kimbo Eucational-United Sound
    Arts, Inc.
10-16 N. Third, Box 477
Long Branch, NJ 07740
(music, physical education,
    dance)

Lakeshore Learning Materials
P.O. Box 6261
Carson, CA 90749
(learning kits, new ideas)

Morrison School Supplies
304 Industrial Way
San Carlos, CA 94070
(learning kits)

Nasco
901 Janesville Avenue
P.O. Box 901
Fort Atkinson, WI 55538-0901
(science materials and kits)

Rhythm Productions/Tom
    Thumb Music
P.O. Box 34485
Los Angeles, CA 90034
(videotapes, cassettes, book
    packages, songwriters)

Rubber Stampede
2542 Tenth Street
Berkeley, CA 94710
(puzzles, games, comic books)

Tada!
120 West 28th Street
New York, NY 10001
(musical plays)

Treehaus Communications, Inc.
906 W. Loveland Avenue
Loveland, OH 45140
(multimedia)

Wards Natural Science, Inc.
P.O. Box 92912
Rochester, NY 14692-9012
(science materials, multimedia,
    computer software)

Warner Press
P.O. Box 2499
Anderson, IN 46018
(coloring and activity books)

EDUCATIONAL MAGAZINE
PUBLISHERS

Arts & Activities
591 Camino de la Reina, Ste.
  200
San Diego, CA 92108

Book Links
50 E. Huron
Chicago, IL 60611

Challenge
Good Apple
Box 299
Carthage, IL 62321-0299

Connect
Teachers' Laboratory, Inc.
28 Birge Street, P.O. Box 6480
Brattleboro, VT 05302-5233

Creative Classroom
Children's Television Workshop
One Lincoln Plaza
New York, NY 10023

Creative Kids
GCT, Inc.
P.O. Box 6448
Mobile, AL 36660-0448

DynaMath
Scholastic, Inc.
730 Broadway
New York, NY 10003

Electronic Learning
Scholastic, Inc.
730 Broadway
New York, NY 10003

The Gifted Child Today
GCT, Inc.
P.O. Box 6448
Mobile, AL 36660-0448

Instructor
Scholastic, Inc.
730 Broadway
New York, NY 10003

Kids Discover
170 Fifth Avenue
New York, NY 10010

Learning93
Springhouse Corporation
P.O. Box 908
Springhouse, PA 19477-0908

Library Talk
5701 N. High Street, Ste. 1
Worthington, OH 43085

Lollipops
Good Apple
Box 299
Carthage, IL 62321-0299

The Mailbox
1607 Battleground Avenue
P.O. Box 97533
Greensboro, NC 27429

Oasis
Good Apple
Box 299
Carthage, IL 62321-0299

Pre-K Today
Scholastic, Inc.
730 Broadway
New York, NY 10003

Schooldays
Frank Schaffer Publications,
   Inc.
23740 Hawthorne Blvd.
Torrance, CA 90509-2853

School Library Journal
249 W. 17th Street
New York, NY 10011

Science Activities
1319 18th Street, NW
Washington, DC 20036-1802

Science and Children
National Science Teacher's Association
1742 Connecticut Avenue, NW
Washington, DC 20009

Science Weekly
2141 Industrial Parkway, Ste.
   202
Silver Springs, MD 20904

SuperScience
Scholastic, Inc.
730 Broadway
New York, NY 10003

Teacher Magazine
4301 Connecticut Avenue, NW
Washington, DC 20008

Teacher's Helper
1607 Battleground Avenue
P.O. Box 97533
Greensboro, NC 27429

Teacher Update
NAR Publication
P.O. Box 12719
Barryville, NY 12719

Teachers & Writers Collaborative
5 Union Square West
New York, NY 10003

Teaching/K–8
40 Richards Avenue
Norwalk, CT 06854

Technology & Learning
2169 East Francisco Boulevard
San Rafael, CA 94901

Wilson Library Bulletin
950 University Avenue
Bronx, NY 10452

Young Children
National Association for Education of Young Children
1509 16th Street, NW
Washington, DC 20036–1426

PARENTING MAGAZINES AND NEWSLETTER MARKETS

(N) newsletter; (NP) newspaper
   format

American Baby Magazine
475 Park Avenue
New York, NY 10016

Bay Area Parent
455 Los Gatos Boulevard
Los Gatos, CA 95023

Building Blocks (N)
38 W. 567 Brindlewood
Elgin, IL 60123

Copycat (NP)
P.O. Box 081546
Racine, WI 53408-1546

Creative Kids
P.O. Box 6448
Mobile, AL 36608

Early Childhood News
2451 River Road
Dayton, OH 45439

Eastside Parent
Northwest Parent Publishing
2107 Elliott Avenue, #303
Seattle, WA 98121

First Teacher
P.O. Box 6781
Syracuse, NY 13217

The Gifted Child Today
P.O. Box 6448
Mobile, AL 36608

Good Apple Newspaper
Box 299
Carthage, IL 62321-0299

Growing Child/Growing Parent
   (N)
22 N. Second Street
P.O. Box 620
Lafayette, IN 47902-0620

Helping Children Learn (NP)
Evan-Moor
18 Lower Ragsdale Drive
Monterey, CA 93940-5746

L.A. Parent
P.O. Box 3204
Burbank, CA 91504

Long Island Parenting News
P.O. Box 214
Island Park, NY 11558

Metrokids Magazine
Kidstuff Publication
2101 Spruce Street
Philadelphia, PA 19103

New York Family
141 Halstead Avenue, Ste. 3D
Mamaroneck, NY 10543

Parentguide News
475 Park Avenue S.
New York, NY 10016

Parenting Magazine
301 Howard, 17th Floor
San Francisco, CA 94105

Parents Magazine
685 Third Avenue
New York, NY 10017

Parent's Digest
100 Park Avenue
New York, NY 10017

Parents' Press
1454 Sixth Street
Berkeley, CA 94710

Seattle's Child
2107 Elliott Avenue, #303
Seattle, WA 98121

Sesame Street Parents' Guide
Children's Television Workshop
One Lincoln Plaza
New York, NY 10023

Today's Family
27 Empire Drive
St. Paul, MN 55103

Totline Newsletter
P.O. Box 2255
Everett, WA 98203

Young Children
NAEYC
1509 16th Street, NW
Washington, DC 20036-1426

RELIGIOUS EDUCATIONAL
MARKETS

*Curriculum and Resource
Materials*

Abingdon Press (Methodist)
201 Eighth Avenue South
P.O. Box 801
Nashville, TN 37202

Accent Books
P.O. Box 15337
Denver, CO 80215

Alpha Omega Publications
P.O. Box 3153
Tempe, AZ 85280

A Beka Book Publications
Textbooks for the Christian
  School
Box 18000
Pensacola, FL 32523-9160

Beacon Hill Press/Nazarene
  Publishing House
The Paseo
Kansas City, MO 64131

Christian Education Publishers
P.O. Box 261129
San Diego, CA 92196

Concordia Publishing House
3558 S. Jefferson Avenue
St. Louis, MO 63118

C.S.S. Publishing Company
628 S. Main Street
Lima, OH 45804

David C. Cook Publishing
  Company
20 Lincoln Avenue
Elgin, IL 60120

Wm. B. Eerdmans Publishing
Company
255 Jefferson Avenue
Grand Rapids, MI 49503

Gospel Light Publishers
2300 Knoll Drive
Ventura, CA 93003

Huntington House Publishers
P.O. Box 53788
Lafayette, LA 70505

Judson Press
P.O. Box 851
Valley Forge, PA 19482-0851

Kar-Ben Copies, Inc. (Judaism)
6800 Tildenwood Lane
Rockville, MD 20852

Liguori Publications (Roman
Catholic)
One Liguori Drive
Liguori, MO 63057-9999

Morehouse Publishing Group
(Episcopal)
871 Ethan Allen Highway,
Ste. 204
Ridgefield, CT 06777

Old Rugged Cross Press
5 Main Street, Ste. 1
Alpharetta, GA 30201

Paulist Press (Roman Catholic)
997 MacArthur Boulevard
Mahaw, NJ 07430

Review and Herald Publishing
Association (Seventh-Day
Adventist)
55 W. Oak Ridge Drive
Hagerstown, MD 21740

Rod and Staff Publishers
(Mennonite)
Highway 172
Crockett, KY 41413

St. Paul Books & Media
50 St. Paul Avenue
Boston, MA 02103

Scripture Press
P.O. Box 650
Glen Ellyn, IL 60138

Shining Star
Division of Good Apple
Box 299
Carthage, IL 62321-0299

Standard Publishing
1821 Hamilton Avenue
Cincinnati, OH 45231

Sunday School of the Southern
Baptist Convention
127 Ninth Avenue N
Nashville, TN 37234

Winston Press
P.O. Box 1630
Hagerstown, MD 21714

Zondervan Publishing House
5300 Patterson SE
Grand Rapids, MI 49530

Magazines

Children's Ministry Magazine
Box 442
Loveland, CO 80539

Christian Education Journal
Scripture Press
P.O. Box 650
Glen Ellyn, IL 60138

Christian Education Today
P.O. Box 15377
Denver, CO 80215

Christian Home and School
3350 E. Paris Avenue SE
Grand Rapids, MI 49512

Christian Parenting Today
P.O. Box 850
Sisters, OR 97759

Church Teachers
1119 Woodburn Road
Durham, NC 27705

The Cross & Quill
Christian Writers Newsletter
P.O. Box 730
DeLand, FL 32721-0730

Evangelizing Today's Child
Warrenton, MO 63383

Home Education Magazine
P.O. Box 1083
Tonaket, WA 98855-1083

Home Life
127 Ninth Avenue N
Nashville, TN 37234

Key to Christian Education
8121 Hamilton Avenue
Cincinnati, OH 45231-2396

Living With Children
127 Ninth Avenue N
Nashville, TN 37234

Living With Preschoolers
127 Ninth Avenue N
Nashville, TN 37234

Living With Teenagers
127 Ninth Avenue N
Nashville, TN 37234

Momentum
National Catholic Educational
    Association
1077 30th Street NW
Washington, DC 20007-3852

The Pedagogic Reporter
A Forum of Jewish Education
730 Broadway
New York, NY 10003

Rod and Staff Newsletter
Highway 173
Crockett, KY 41413

Teaching Home
P.O. Box 20219
Portland, OR 97220-0219

Today's Catholic Teacher
2451 E. River Road
Dayton, OH 45439-1597

Today's Christian Woman
465 Gundersen Drive
Carol Stream, IL 60188

RESOURCE BOOKS FOR AUTHORS

Brande, Dorothea, *Becoming a Writer,* St. Martin's Press

Bowker, *Subject Guide to Children's Books in Print*

Bronfeld, Stewart, *Writing for Film and Television,* Touchstone/S&S

Burack, Abraham, *Writer's Handbook,* The Writer

Carpenter, Lisa, *Children's Writer's and Ilustrator's Market,* Writer's Digest Books

Chicago Manual of Style, University of Chicago Press

Commire, Anne, editor, *Something About the Author,* Gale Research

Conner, Susan, editor, *Artist's Market,* Writer's Digest

Gale Research, *Book Review Index*

Giblin, James Cross, *Writing Books for Young People,* The Writer

Harmon, Renée, *The Beginning Filmmaker's Business Guide,* Walker

Kissling, Mark, Editor, *Writer's Market,* Writer's Digest

Litowinsky, Olga, *Writing and Publishing Books for Children in the 1990s,* Walker

Orenstein, Vik, *Creative Techniques for Photographing Children,* Writer's Digest Books

Philips, Christopher Lee, *A Guide to the College Library,* Walker

Polking, Kirk, *A Beginner's Guide to Getting Published,* Writer's Digest

Strunk, William, Jr., and White, E. B. *The Elements of Style,* Macmillan.

Seuling, Barbara, *How to Write a Children's Book and Get It Published,* Scribners.

Wolff, Jurgen, *Successful Scriptwriting,* Writer's Digest

Shulevtz, Uri, *Writing With Pictures,* Watson-Guptill

Yolen, Jane, *Guide to Writing for Children,* The Writer

EDUCATIONAL ASSOCIATIONS
AND ORGANIZATIONS

American Educational Research Journal
College of Education
University of Maryland
College Park, MD 20742

Association for Childhood Education International
11141 Georgia Avenue, Ste. 200
Wheaton, MD 20902

Association of Christian Schools International
P.O. Box 4097
Whittier, CA 90607–4097

Association of Jewish Book Publishers
192 Lexington Avenue
New York, NY 10016–6801

Association of Journalists and Authors
1501 Broadway, Ste. 302
New York, NY 10036

Association for Supervision and Curriculum Development
1250 N. Pitt Street
Alexandria, VA 22341

Catholic Book Publisher's Association
333 Glen Head Road
Old Brookfield, NY 11545

Christian Home Educators Association
P.O. Box 2009
Norwalk, CA 90651–2001

College English Association
English Department
Youngstown State University
Youngstown, OH 44555

Evangelical Church Library
  Association
P.O. Box 3353
Glen Ellyn, IL 60138

Lutheran Church Library Association
122 W. Franklin
Minneapolis, MN 55404

Friends of the Library
1326 Spruce Street, Ste. 1105
Philadelphia, PA 19107

Graphic Artists Guild, Inc.
11 W. 20th Street, 8th Floor
New York, NY 10011

International Reading Association
800 Barksdale Road
Newark, DE 19711

Journal of Learning Disabilities
Department of Special
  Education
University of Texas
Austin, TX 78712-1290

Lutheran Educational
  Association
7400 Augusta
River Forest, IL 60305

National Art Education Association
1916 Association Drive
Reston, VA 22091

National Association for Day
  Care
725 15th Street NW, Ste. 505
Washington, DC 20005

National Association for Gifted
  Children
1155 15th Street NW, #1002
Washington, DC 20005

National Association of Education
1201 16th Street NW
Washington, DC 20036

National Association of Independent Schools
75 Federal
Boston, MA 02110

National Association of Parish
  Coordinators/Directors of
  Religious Education
1077 30th Street, Ste. 100
Washington, DC 20007-3852

National Association of Patent
  Attorneys
2001 Jefferson Drive Highway,
  Ste. 203
Arlington, VA 22202

National Association of School
Art and Design
11250 Roger Bacon Drive,
#21
Reston, VA 22090

National Association of Science
Writers
P.O. Box 294
Greenlawn, NY 11740

National Catholic Educational
Association
1077 30th Street NW, Ste. 100
Washington, DC 20007

National Child Day Care Association
1501 Benning Road, NW
Washington, DC 20002

National Council for the Social
Studies
3501 Newark Street NW
Washington, DC 20016

National Council of Teachers of
Education
1111 Kenyon Road
Urbana, IL 61801

National Council of Teachers of
English
1111 Kenyon Road
Urbana, IL 61801

National Head Start Association
201 N. Union Street, Ste. 320
Alexandria, VA 22314

National League of American
Pen Women
1300 17th Street NW
Washington, DC 20036

National Parent Teacher Association
700 North Rush Street
Chicago, IL 60611-2571

National School Supply and
Equipment Association
8300 Colesville, Ste. 250
Silver Springs, MD 20910

National Science Teachers Association
1742 Connecticut Avenue NW
Washington, DC 20009

National Speakers Association
1500 S. Priest Drive, Ste. 350
Tempe, AZ 85281

National Writers Club
1450 S. Havana, Ste. 620
Aurora, CO 80012

The New Advocate
125 Alderhold Hall
University of Georgia
Athens, GA 30602

Otis Art Institute
Parsons School of Design
2401 Wilshire Boulevard
Los Angeles, CA 90065

Public Relations Society of
    America
33 Irving Place, 3rd Floor
New York, NY 10003–2376

Society of Children's Book
    Writers and Illustrators
22736 Vanowen Street, Ste. 106
West Hills, CA 91307

Society of Illustrators
128 E. 63rd Street
New York, NY 10021

Teachers and Writers Magazine
5 Union Square West
New York, NY 10003

Textbook Authors Association
Box 535
Orange Springs, FL 32182

Toastmaster's Club International
P.O. Box 9052
Mission Viejo, CA 92690

Washington Independent
    Writers
220 Woodward Building
733 15th Street NW
Washington, DC 20005

Writers Guild of America
8955 Beverly Boulevard
W. Hollywood, CA 90048

INDEX